The Higher Civil Service in Britain

in Britain

Richard A. Chapman

Senior Lecturer,
Institute of Local Government Studies,
University of Birmingham

Constable London

First published in 1970
by Constable and Co Ltd
10 Orange Street London WC2
Copyright © 1970 by Richard A. Chapman
All rights reserved
Printed in Great Britain by
The Anchor Press Ltd, and bound by
Wm. Brendon & Son Ltd, both of Tiptree, Essex
ISBN 0 09 455620 2

SOCIOLOGY AND SOCIAL WELFARE SERIES

edited by Paul Halmos

The Higher Civil Service in Britain

Contents

Acknowledgments

I should like to thank the following for permission to quote from the works stated: Cambridge University Press for Sir Edward Bridges' *Portrait of a Profession, The Civil Service Tradition*; Encounter Ltd for Andrew Shonfield's 'The Pragmatic Illusion', published in *Encounter*, June 1967; The Clarendon Press for H. E. Dale's *The Higher Civil Service of Great Britain*; William Heinemann Ltd for C. K. Munro's *The Fountains in Trafalgar Square*; Constable and Co Ltd for Graham Wallas' *Human Nature in Politics*; Her Majesty's Stationery Office for the MacDonnell, Tomlin, and Priestley Royal Commission Reports on the Civil Service, the Report (and supporting volumes) of the Fulton Committee, and the Report of the Royal Commission on Oxford and Cambridge Universities; Macdonald and Co Ltd for William Reid's 'Civil Service', published in Robin Guthrie (Ed.), *Outlook, a Careers Symposium*; and the Editor, *Public Administration*, for Edward Hughes' 'Civil Service Reform 1853–5', published in *Public Administration*, Vol. 32, 1954.

Preface

This book combines analysis and discussion with a descriptive account of important aspects of the higher Civil Service in Britain. After tracing the origins and development of the Service, it concentrates on how some of the most significant decision-makers in the country are recruited, how they go about their daily work, what training they receive and what they like and dislike about their work. It is also concerned with relations between Civil Service classes, how the processes of administration proceed and how officials are accommodated in government buildings. There is a chapter on the private life, political attitudes and social backgrounds of higher civil servants. It is the first book devoted to such a general survey of the higher Civil Service since H. E. Dale, in the 1930s, wrote his classic study covering many of the same topics from the viewpoint of a recently retired senior official in the Ministry of Agriculture and Fisheries.

The book grew primarily out of some work I was commissioned to do for the Fulton Committee on the Civil Service. It was a great privilege to do that research, for it constituted the first survey of its kind into the work and attitudes of Administrative Class civil servants in Britain, and I am very grateful to everyone who helped. I should particularly like to record my thanks for their encouragement and assistance to the late Professor Lord Simey, Dr Norman Hunt, Mr R. W. L. Wilding and Mr M. A. Simons. The research would not have been possible without the good-humoured co-operation of the 1956 direct entrants into the Administrative Class who answered a lengthy questionnaire (containing fifty-eight questions and often taking up to four hours to complete) and endured a follow-up interview (lasting, on average, an hour and a half) during which I asked more questions and tried out some of my ideas.

For their help in reading and commenting on an earlier draft of this book I should like to thank Professor Wilfrid Harrison, Professor Paul Halmos, Dr J. D. Stewart, Mr Richard Butt, Mr Peter Dixon and Mr R. W. L. Wilding. For typing assistance I should like to thank

the Department of Local Government and Administration in the
University of Birmingham; and for help in drawing up the index,
Mrs Gael Heller.

Introduction

'. . . the invention of a competitive Civil Service . . .
took its place in our habitual political psychology.
We now half-consciously conceive of the Civil Service
as an unchanging fact whose good and bad points are
to be taken or left as a whole.'[1]

The 'higher Civil Service' is a vague term which is in general use
partly because it has the advantages of imprecision and partly because
it had a more specific meaning in the past. It is a term in keeping with
the traditions of British government, used mainly by people who
feel they 'know' its meaning and who feel that others will also 'know'
when it is used. For the cognoscenti it does not need to be defined
and to them this book may therefore appear superfluous.

This book is not, however, primarily intended for the cognoscenti
but for people who want a better understanding of certain aspects of
central government in Britain. It is the first general sociological
survey of the higher Civil Service since H. E. Dale wrote his classic
study[2] from the inside point of view in the 1930s.

THE PROBLEM OF DEFINITION

Dale was a retired civil servant whose principal object in writing
his book was 'to offer some account of the highest section of the
Home Civil Service, numerically a tiny proportion of the whole,
and of the functions which they in fact discharge day by day within
one part of their region of labour, the field of policy'. He was concerned with 'the men at or near the top', 'the "governing classes" ',
who have a voice in deciding what is to be done in public affairs of
importance. Yet Dale found it difficult to be more precise about
what is meant by 'the higher Civil Service'.

He explained that he meant 'the relatively few officials, usually
at or near the head of their departments, who are in a position to
exercise a real and direct influence upon government policy in

important matters'. He recognised how difficult it was to formulate a more exact description and that two of the main weaknesses in his own concerned the meaning of the phrases 'who are in a position to exercise' and 'important matters'.

Later writers have had to face the same problem and have not been conspicuously more successful than Dale. R. K. Kelsall, for example, in his study of higher civil servants, concentrated on those of Assistant Secretary grade or above because 'in the hierarchy of the Civil Service, authority to take policy decisions does not normally attach to those below the rank of Assistant Secretary'.[3] But according to T. A. Critchley, 'the higher Civil Service comprises the cream of the Administrative Class: a variable number of Principals, together with the Assistant Secretaries, Under Secretaries, Deputy Secretaries and heads of Departments'.[4]

The study of public administration or government does not in general claim to be a precise science with elements all of which can be measured with mathematical precision, and it is not surprising that a study of part of it should also involve aspects which cannot be measured. It would be foolish without good reason to expect an academic discipline to be precise in a way that it does not claim to be. Thus it is not possible to measure exactly the number of people in the higher Civil Service at any one time. Indeed, the task of being more specific is fraught with difficulties.

The first difficulty concerns the basic meaning of the term, the Civil Service. There is still no more precise definition than that adopted by the Tomlin and Priestley Royal Commissions on the Civil Service:[5] 'those servants of the Crown, other than holders of political or judicial offices, who are employed in a civil capacity, and whose remuneration is paid wholly and directly out of monies voted by Parliament'. Although not entirely satisfactory, this standard definition has been accepted by nearly all writers on the Civil Service since that time. For most purposes this is an adequate definition.

However, it does give rise to certain difficulties, and W. J. M. Mackenzie and J. W. Grove[6] have already made some comments about them.

They have pointed out that 'servants of the Crown' is a phrase of little use in deciding marginal cases (such as Regional Hospital Boards) whose statutory position in this respect is uncertain and has not yet been cleared up by judicial decision. Furthermore, if it is held that a particular public corporation is a 'servant of the Crown' it will follow that its employees are 'servants of the Crown', but it does not in fact follow that its employees are civil servants. Just how fine a distinction this can be, and also how confusing, is seen when the position of the Post Office is considered in relation to the Civil Service. In 1969 it became a public corporation and for almost all purposes its employees ceased to be civil servants – although they continued performing the same functions, and the change in status of the organization hardly affected the general public at all.

'Holders of political office' can now be defined by reference to the House of Commons Disqualification Act, 1957. But until that Act was passed the phrase could be defined only by reference to the practice of the House of Commons in interpreting clauses in the Regency Act of 1705 and in later Acts which excluded the holders of certain offices from sitting as members of the House of Commons: offices which did not exclude were then political offices.

The phrase 'holders of judicial office' presents difficulties because the courts have had to decide when an employee is bound to act judicially.

While 'employment in a civil capacity' is quite definite in a negative way, as it covers employment other than in the armed forces, 'remuneration paid wholly and directly out of monies voted by Parliament' is probably the most important part of the definition. A 'servant of the Crown' may be remunerated 'directly but not wholly' if he works for a government Department part-time. Thus a man working one day a month for a retaining fee might be in law a 'crown servant' that day, but he could scarcely be called a 'part-time civil servant'.

'Directly' is also important as it excludes servants of the Crown (such as those working for the British Council) who are paid by monies issued indirectly as a grant-in-aid, and not from the normal form of Parliamentary grant.

After outlining these aspects of the meaning of the term, it is necessary to explain that the Civil Service, as defined, may be considered in various ways. There is the Home Civil Service and the Diplomatic Service. There are industrial civil servants and non-industrial civil servants. This book is not concerned with the industrial civil servants – who are employed in establishments like the Royal Dockyards – and it is only concerned from time to time with the Diplomatic Service. The main concern is the higher levels within the non-industrial Home Civil Service.

TABLE I[7]

NON-INDUSTRIAL STAFF IN THE HOME CIVIL SERVICE ON 1ST
JANUARY 1968

Staff Group	Permanent*	Temporary †	Total	Per cent of whole
Administrative	2,624	160	2,784‡	0·4
Executive (general and departmental	87,907	3,159	91,066	12·0
Clerical officers (general and departmental)	117,308	22,869	140,177	18·5
Clerical assistants	35,419	53,849	89,268	11·7
Typing	11,079	18,880	29,959	3·9
Inspectorate	2,785	93	2,878	0·4
Messengerial	19,039	16,361	35,400	4·7
Post Office minor and manipulative	182,961	42,090	225,051	29·7
Professional, scientific and technical I	20,518	6,000	26,518	3·5
Scientific and technical II	42,343	16,803	59,146	7·8
Ancillary, technical and miscellaneous supervisory grades etc.	38,085	17,877	55,962	7·4
Total	560,068	198,141	758,209	100·0

* Central Staff Record figures.

† From departmental returns.

‡ Nearly 300 more than the overall total of those in the various grades in the Administrative Class, largely due to the inclusion here of certain civil servants more appropriate to the administrative than to other groups in this table.

Notes: Diplomatic Service staff at home and abroad (5,223 permanent and 1,396 temporary) and Post Office engineering etc. staff formerly classified as industrial (92,415 permanent and 21,382 temporary) are excluded from the above figures. Home Departments' staff serving abroad are included, but not locally engaged staff. Part-timers totalling 44,774 have been counted as half. The total for the non-industrial Home Civil Service excluding the Post Office was 465,000 on 1st January 1968.

Home civil servants may be further divided according to their broad Classes (such as Administrative, Professional and Scientific, Executive, Clerical) and within each Class they may be sub-divided according to their level in the hierarchy. The numbers of non-industrial staff in the Home Civil Service on 1st January 1968 were as shown in Table I.

The Class with highest status in the Service is the Administrative Class, whose essential function is, according to the Association of First Division Civil Servants, 'to bring together the disparate issues involved in taking major decisions of policy, to advise on what these decisions should be and subsequently to put them into effect'.[8] Its members are divided into the six main grades as shown in Table II:

TABLE II[9]

NUMBERS AND GRADES IN THE ADMINISTRATIVE CLASS

	Numbers at 1.4.67			Pay at 1.1.70 £ a year
	Permanent	Temporary	Total	
Joint Permanent Secretary to the Treasury and Secretary to the Cabinet	3	—	3	10,400
Permanent Secretary	18	—	18	9,800
Second Permanent Secretary	7	—	7	9,300
Deputy Secretary	72	—	72	7,100
Under Secretary	270	2	272	6,125*
Assistant Secretary	798	4	802	4,170–5,325*
Principal	1,001	65	1,066	2,724–3,721*
Assistant Principal	255	3	258	1,196–1,952*
Total	2,424	74	2,498	

* Includes £125 London allowance.

Notes: (i) In Departments where the Ministerial head is known as the Secretary of State, titles of grades above Assistant Secretary become Assistant Under Secretary of State, Deputy Under Secretary of State and Permanent Under Secretary of State respectively.

(ii) Assistant Principals receive a special increase of £144 on completion of probation, normally after two years' service.

These figures are given so that the higher Civil Service, however defined, may be seen in numerical perspective. Although most of this book will be dealing with the Administrative Class (Dale considered only the grade of Assistant Secretary and above as coming within his category of those 'who are in a position to exercise a real and direct influence upon government policy'), from time to time others, such as senior specialists in the Professional and Scientific Class, who number about 500, will also be considered. The fact remains, however, that most of those generally considered to be higher civil servants are in the Administrative Class which constitutes only about one half per cent of the whole non-industrial Civil Service. Also, the term 'higher Civil Service' seems now, by general consensus, to be equated with the Administrative Class and in particular with the higher levels within it. In the nineteenth century, the term had a more precise meaning because before 1890 the terms 'Higher Division' and 'Lower Division' were used to distinguish the small number of civil servants primarily engaged in intellectual work from the larger number engaged in routine work.

In 1955 the Priestley Royal Commission formulated a precise definition for 'the higher Civil Service'. It stated that in using the term it means 'all staffs whose salary maximum or whose fixed rate exceeds the maximum of the Principal'.[10] But that definition has been subsequently accepted only inside the Service for technical purposes of administration (for example, the 1969 Report of the Committee on the pay of higher civil servants[11] seems to have accepted that definition): it has not been more generally accepted. For most purposes both within and outside the Service the term is equated with the Administrative Class because it is regarded as having the dominant role.

Until recently remarkably little had been published about higher civil servants. Little had been written about what they do, how they are trained for their important duties, or how they go about their work: even less was known about such matters as their attitudes to work, political allegiance or religious affiliation. Such writings as did exist depended mainly on memoirs by retired civil servants or the somewhat arid descriptions in careers literature of typical work in certain grades and classes (often potentially misleading because of the variety of work in the higher Civil Service). There were a number of reasons for this, including restrictions imposed by the Official Secrets

Acts, the traditional reticence of civil servants and the delicacy and difficulties of writing authoritatively about such matters – most of the facts were not available even through the official records (which tended to be out of date and from which there was never staff available to make a reliable analysis).

Many of these difficulties still exist, but in the last five years there has been a welcome relaxation of information of various sorts. There has been greater freedom for civil servants who wish to do so to write and talk about their work. And the Fulton Committee, which reported in 1968, helped shed light on the subject by publishing official information collected for it from within the Service, and by sponsoring a small number of research studies which looked at various aspects of Civil Service work and the individuals involved in it, in ways never before attempted.

Although a considerable amount of material has been released in the virtually six volumes of evidence published in support of the Fulton Report, it has not so far been conveniently arranged to focus attention on any level of Civil Service work from a broad sociological viewpoint. This study is an attempt to provide such a comprehensive picture in a single volume by re-analysing all the information available on the higher Civil Service and presenting it together with a certain amount of information published here for the first time.

B

2. Outline of Development

'The creation of this Service was the great political invention in nineteenth-century England, and like other inventions it was worked out under the pressure of an urgent practical problem.'[1]

The basic structure of the Civil Service in Britain was laid in the last century in the Report on the Organization of the Permanent Civil Service, 1854 (the Northcote-Trevelyan Report). This in turn had been inspired by the genius of Macaulay, who was responsible for the new Civil Service for India.

For an understanding of the principles on which the British Civil Service has been selected, trained, and organized since the mid-nineteenth century, it is necessary first to consider the reforms in the Indian Civil Service. These helped provide a stimulus for administrative reform at home, and their architect presented a philosophy which has been found relevant for other fields as well.

The essential feature of the philosophy was clearly stated in the words of the Report on the Indian Civil Service: 'We believe that men who have been engaged up to twenty-one or twenty-two in studies which have no immediate connection with the business of any profession, and of which the effect is merely to open, to invigorate, and to enrich the mind, will generally be found, in the business of every profession, superior to men who have, at eighteen or nineteen, devoted themselves to the special studies of their calling'.[2]

THE INDIAN CIVIL SERVICE

From early in the seventeenth century up to 1858, British sovereignty over India was exercised through a corporation known as 'the Company' (strictly speaking it was 'the governor and company of merchants of London trading into the East Indies'). It was a body of private persons whose objects were to send trading ships to the East Indies and to establish there trading-posts with the permission of the local

8

rulers. In 1709 the London company was swallowed up by a new body known as the 'united company of merchants of England trading to the East Indies' and from 1833 this was shortened to the 'East India Company'.

Although it was originally a trading company, it gradually acquired territories, introduced the rule of law, and was transformed from a commercial corporation into a government.[3] Its employees became administrators instead of traders and were referred to as its 'civil servants' to distinguish them from its army, navy and ecclesiastical employees. The term 'civil service' thus originates from the East India Company and it was only slowly that the technical phrase of the Anglo-Indian was adopted for home use.[4]

Servants of the Company were commonly recruited as writers, on the nomination of a director, and sent to India at sixteen years of age, though some were younger and Henry Vansittart is believed to have been only thirteen when his father sent him out. It took about six or seven months to reach India and the chances of the recruits seeing home again were not so good as those of a young man leaving for the trenches in the First World War. As writers in the Honourable East India Company's Service (they wrote H.E.I.C.S. after their names) they spent most of their time copying letters and checking cargoes.

But responsibility soon came. Hastings at twenty was organizing a sub-factory for collecting and winding raw silk; at twenty-five he was conducting negotiations between the Nawab and Governor Roger Drake, and at twenty-seven he was President at Mir Jafar's Court, perhaps the second post in Bengal. Vansittart had been appointed President of the Council and Governor of Fort William when he was reputed to be only twenty-eight.

Phillip Woodruff has explained that such men 'were faced with a complex civilization, with thirty million or so of subtle and intelligent people, professing one or two ancient religions whose sacred books the English could not read. Their law was strange to the English and in practice was seldom observed; their institutions were overlaid and obscured by the dust of invading cavalry and the mould of despotism in decay. To this vast, this almost infinite, mass of incomprehensible material a few of the English from the start bent themselves laboriously and set about the task of understanding, straightening and controlling – a task that seems as hopeless and unending as any devised by witch for the humiliation of transformed princess.'[5]

Sir Edward Blunt has explained that one of the special characteristics of the I.C.S. was the great variety of duties which its members performed: '. . . the administrator in his district was wont, as part of his ordinary work, to build his own roads and canals and bridges, to dig his own wells, to manage his own jail, and to act as his own sanitary inspector. And any civilian might be called on to serve one or other of such an assortment of offices as those of policeman, postmaster, surveyor, customs officer, educationist, stamp vendor, salt agent, lottery superintendent, auditor, paymaster of troops, and even banker.'[6]

'In a list of Bengal civil servants from 1780 to 1838, there are to be found the names of many posts which are still familiar, though they often appear in curious combinations. Such are board of revenue, commissioner, collector, magistrate and district judge. There is also a galaxy of secretaries, with their deputies and assistants, in various departments – revenue and judicial; political, foreign and secret; military; public; general; financial; Persian – with chief and private secretaries. There are also many posts which are now the preserve of special departments, though to some of them the civilian still has access – audit and accounts, police, political, opium, post office, stamps and jails.

'The list includes some curious posts. One is "endorser of stamp papers" – naturally, a junior appointment. Another is "vendor and distributor of stamps" – which nowadays is reserved for a treasury clerk. A third is "superintendent of botanical gardens", whilst one officer is appointed "to devote his time entirely to the trial of Thuggs"; and as it was his last post, he must have found enough Thuggs to fill up his time for the rest of his service. Another, having spent twenty-one years as a judge, became a postmaster-general; a third, having been seven years in the police, became a judge of the *sadr* court; and a fourth, after spending many years in high posts in the customs department, became a joint magistrate. One scents a sensation here.'[7]

These first civil servants received no proper training, they spent the first year or so of their employment as copyists and then were appointed to particular posts and learned their duties as they carried them out. This was the only way to learn the various duties of such appointments in India at that time and the Company realised it.

The only educational qualification for entry into the service was, until 1800 (long after the duties of the Company's servants had ceased to be purely commercial), the rudiments of commercial knowledge. Lord Wellesley was the first to perceive that much more than this was needed and he founded a residential college at Fort William which all new civil servants had to attend.

The course at Fort William was planned to last three years and the curriculum was to include Indian history, law, religion, ethnology and oriental languages, ethics, civil jurisprudence, international law and general history. But Wellesley's plans were not fully realised as the directors of the Company regarded them as unnecessarily elaborate and expensive and refused to approve of anything more than the maintenance of the college as a school of oriental languages. The college ceased to be residential in 1835 and was abolished in 1854, by which time it had outlived its usefulness.

However, the directors were persuaded by some of Wellesley's arguments and in 1806 they founded a college in England, which was first housed at Hertford Castle, and in 1809 moved to Haileybury. The age of admission was originally fifteen, but was raised in 1833 to a minimum of seventeen and a maximum of twenty years. Four years later the maximum became twenty-one years, but the limits of age for admission remained at seventeen to twenty-one until the college was abolished in 1857. The curriculum included oriental languages and literature, mathematics, natural history, classical and general literature, law, history and political economy. The course lasted two years.

' "The object of this establishment", says the prospectus of 1806, "is to provide a supply of persons duly qualified to discharge the various and important duties required from civil servants of the Company in administering the government in India." The college achieved its object. It produced men who as members of the civil service, realised that "there were certain traditions to be kept up and handed over . . . a political faith to be cherished, and a code of public and private honour to be rigidly maintained." '[8]

The Company's charter came up for renewal every twenty years, and when the 1813 Bill was being considered Lord Grenville suggested that the Company should change its methods of recruitment to the service from nomination by directors to competitive selection. His suggestion was not then adopted, but as a move towards it the Charter Act of 1833 laid down that the directors should nominate annually three times as many candidates as there were vacancies. By this method four young men were nominated for each vacancy and there was a competitive examination to decide which of them was the best; but it lasted for only a year.

It was during the debate on the 1833 India Bill that T. B. Macaulay (later Lord Macaulay) won his spurs as a Minister. He was then Secretary of the Board of Control and responsible for the clauses which sought to establish a system of appointment by competition. The passage in his speech where he explained and defended these clauses has since been quoted (and mis-quoted) many times as a significant step in the development of the principle of open competition as a method of recruitment to public offices. Macaulay said:

'. . . It is said, I know, that examinations in Latin, in Greek and in mathematics are no tests of what men will prove to be in life. I am perfectly aware that they are not infallible tests; but that they are tests I confidently maintain. Look at every walk of life – at this House – at the other House – at the Bar – at the Bench – at the Church – and see whether it be not true, that those who attain high distinction in the world are generally men who were distinguished in their academic career. Indeed, Sir, this objection would prove far too much even for those who use it. It would prove, that there is no use at all in education. Why should we put boys out of their way? Why should we force a lad, who would much rather fly a kite or trundle a hoop, to learn his Latin Grammar? Why should we keep a young man to his Thucydides or his Laplace, when he would much rather be shooting? Education would be mere useless torture, if, at two or three and twenty, a man who has neglected his studies were exactly on a par with a man who has applied himself to them – exactly as likely to perform all the offices of public life with credit to himself and with advantage to society. Whether the English system of education be good or bad is not now the question. Perhaps I may think that too much time is given to the ancient languages and to the abstract sciences. But what then? Whatever be the languages – whatever be the sciences, which it is, in any age or country, the fashion to teach, those who become the greatest proficients in those languages, and those sciences will generally be the flower of the youth – the most astute – the most industrious – the most ambitious of honourable distinctions. If the Ptolemaic system were taught at Cambridge, instead of the Newtonian, the senior wrangler would nevertheless be in general a superior man to the wooden spoon. If, instead of learning Greek, we learned the Cherokee, the man who understood the Cherokee best, who made the most correct and melodious Cherokee verses – who comprehended most accurately the effect of the Cherokee particles – would generally be a superior man to him who was destitute of these accomplishments. If astrology were taught at our Universities, the young man who cast nativities best would generally turn out a superior man. If alchymy were taught, the young man who showed most activity in the pursuit of the philosopher's stone, would generally turn out a superior man.'[9]

By the Charter Act of 1833 the Company ceased altogether to be a commercial body, though it retained its administrative and political powers 'in trust for His Majesty, his heirs and successors, for the service of the government of India'. Thus from 1833 until 1858, when its long connection with India came to an end, the Company's sole concern was the government of its territories.

In 1853 Macaulay's views prevailed, and the last Charter Act abolished the practice of recruitment through nomination by directors; instead appointments were to be thrown open to competition.

A committee was appointed to advise on the best method of carrying them out. Its chairman was Lord Macaulay and two of its members were the Rev. H. Melvill (then Principal of Haileybury) and the Rev. Benjamin Jowett (of Balliol College, Oxford). The Report was brief, but to the point – Macaulay wrote it himself during the first week of July 1854.[10]

The committee recommended the abolition of Haileybury, a period of probation for all candidates successful at the competitive examination and the principle that this examination 'should be so conducted as to ensure the selection of candidates with thorough, and not merely superficial knowledge' (this last recommendation was made in the hope of defeating the crammer).

Before 1906, candidates could take as many subjects as they chose out of a wide range. This had unfortunate results for candidates who, however talented, felt it in their interests to go to a crammer, for at the end of the nineteenth century crammers would boast that a man who came for six weeks could gain an additional 500 marks. After 1906, however, the rules were altered so that no candidate could offer more subjects than would command a total of 6,000 marks.

Most of the recruits to the Indian Civil Service by the system of

TABLE III[11]

PROFESSIONS AND OCCUPATIONS OF THE FATHERS OF THE
CANDIDATES WHO PASSED THEIR 'FURTHER' OR 'FINAL'
EXAMINATIONS, AND WERE CERTIFICATED FOR THE CIVIL
SERVICE OF INDIA DURING THE 15 YEARS, 1860–1874

	number	per cent
Honourable; Baronet; Gentleman; J.P. and D.L; Landed Proprietor; of no profession	67	10·0
Officers of the Army (44); Navy (3); French Army (1); Civil Service (16); Ambassador (1)	65	9·8
Clergymen (Church of England and Ireland) (145); other Ministers of Religion and Missionaries (39)	184	27·5
India Civil Service (47); Colonial Civil Service (7); Zemindar; Planter; Irish J.P. residing in Natal	57	8·5
Law: Barristers; Magistrates; County Court Judge (20); Solicitor; Notary; Clerk to the Peace, etc (29)	49	7·4
Medicine: Physicians; Surgeons	65	9·7
Merchant (38); Banker (4); Manufacturer (2); Shipowner (1); Stockbroker (1); Wine Merchant (2)	48	7·2
Architect and Engineer	11	1·7
President of College; Professor; Schoolmaster	27	4·0
Secretary; Agent; Manager; Librarian (1); Cashier of Steam Packet Company (1); Accountant (2); Officer in the Merchant Service (1); Commission Agent (1)	20	3·0
Farmer (17); Land Agent (7); Miller (2); Woolstapler (1); Assistant to County Surveyor (1)	28	4·2
Baker (1); Butcher (1); Chemist and Druggist (2); Bookseller, Printer, Printseller, Stationer (6); Tailor, Draper (7); Shoemaker (1); Ironmonger, 'Wright' (3); Upholsterer, Undertaker (3); Cheese Factor (1); Confectioner (1); Licensed Victualler (1)	27	4·0
Organist (1); Merchant's Clerk; Railway Clerk (2); Steward; Gamekeeper (2); Station Master (1)	6	·9
Not specified	14	2·1
Total	668	100

The social position of the competitioners may also be inferred from the schools or other places of education which they have attended. Taking as the best evidence on this point the facts of the most recent examination, it appears that, of the first 40 candidates in order of merit at the competition of 1874, the number educated at public schools was 30, of whom 14 proceeded to some University. Of the residue, 4 attended at some University or college who had not previously been at any public school.

open competition came from the higher social classes. In fact, of the 668 civilians sent out to India between 1860 and 1874, 78 per cent were the sons of parents belonging to the aristocracy, gentry, army, navy, Indian Civil Service, or one of the learned professions; most of them were about twenty years of age. Examples are given in Tables III, IV, V and VI.

TABLE IV[12]

BIRTHPLACES OF THE 741 SUCCESSFUL COMPETITORS FOR THE INDIA CIVIL SERVICE WHO PROCEEDED TO INDIA BETWEEN 1855 AND 1874

England	350
Scotland	89
Ireland	156
Guernsey	3
France (3); Belgium (1); Germany (3); Austria (1); Russia (1)	9
Gibraltar, St Helena, Ascension	3
India and Ceylon (7 of Indian races included)	102
Mauritius (4); Penang; China	6
Canada, New Brunswick, Red River Settlement	4
West Indies	11
United States; Brazil	2
Tasmania (3); Polynesia (2)	5
At Sea	1
Total	741

THE RELEVANCE OF THE I.C.S. AND OTHER CONTEMPORARY REFORMS

For the purposes of this present study, the I.C.S. can be regarded as having two significant characteristics. One characteristic was the great variety of the duties which its members performed, and the long periods which they spent touring among the people. There were practically no duties which were outside the scope of the I.C.S. except those of the sailor, the soldier, the physician and the padre, and there were occasions when the civilian occasionally performed some of even these duties, in an amateur way. As time passed, and administration became more complex, the government was forced to

TABLE V[13]

AGES OF CANDIDATES SELECTED DURING THE 16 YEARS, 1859
TO 1874

Year	Limits of age in force	Number of candidates selected who were						Total number of candidates selected
		over 17	over 18	over 19	over 20	over 21	over 22	
1859	18—23*	—	1	3	9	13	14	40
1860	18—22	—	8	16	29	27	—	80
1861	18—22	—	11	15	32	22	—	80
1862	18—22	—	13	15	23	29	—	80
1863	18—22	—	20	9	12	19	—	60
1864	18—22	—	10	11	8	11	—	40
1865	17—22	—	4	8	26	12	—	50
1866	17—21	2	4	20	24	—	—	50
1867	17—21	1	8	14	27	—	—	50
1868	17—21	2	8	16	25	—	—	51
1869	17—21	2	3	13	32	—	—	50
1870	17—21	1	4	14	21	—	—	40
1871	17—21	—	4	6	25	—	—	35
1872	17—21	2	5	9	20	—	—	36
1873	17—21	—	6	8	21	—	—	35
1874	17—21	3	7	10	20	—	—	40
Total		13	116	187	354	133	14	817

* *i.e.*, 'above 18 and under 23'.

create a number of technical departments, each with its staff of specially trained experts who took over many of the civilian's former
duties. But there always remained a number of departments which
were then non-technical and to which civilians were appointed and
put in charge (these included customs, ports and telegraphs, agriculture, co-operative credit, census, etc). The whole position was aptly
summarised by Sir Edward Blunt when he said: 'No civilian need
ever fear that his work will lack variety.'

The other special characteristic was that the i.c.s. was a silent
and anonymous service. It was rarely mentioned in the newspapers
unless something had gone wrong, or seemed likely to go wrong.

TABLE VI[14]

NUMBER OF SUCCESSFUL COMPETITORS OF THE LAST FIVE
YEARS (1870–4), WHO CAME DIRECT FROM SCHOOL OR COLLEGE
WITHOUT SPECIAL PREPARATION

The total number of successful competitors in the years 1870–4	186
Of these 44 came up without special preparation, viz.:	
From Oxford	7
Cambridge	8
London University	
University and King's Colleges	5
Wesley College, Sheffield	1
Edinburgh	3
Aberdeen	1
Trinity College, Dublin	4
Queen's University in Ireland	6
Cheltenham College	6
Liverpool Institute	2
Blackheath Proprietary School	1
	44

In many of the other cases the amount of special preparation was comparatively trifling.

From time to time some admirer in Parliament or in the press or on a public platform made complimentary remarks about it. Consequently, the general public knew little about what it actually did and the sort of lives its servants led – all this was consistent with the best traditions of the Victorian period.

Both these characteristics are important because they are similar to characteristics of the Home Civil Service and have in recent years been focal points for criticism of the contemporary Civil Service. These matters will be further discussed in subsequent chapters.

Apart from a number of similarities between the problems and suggested solutions for the i.c.s. and the Home Civil Service, the Indian experience is also important for two other reasons. It reflected and drew upon the nineteenth century reforms in the Universities of Oxford and Cambridge, and the names of people responsible there are closely connected with reforms of the Home Civil Service.

The reform movement in both Oxford and Cambridge began within the universities about the turn of the century – for example, at Cambridge the reforms are said[15] to have begun in 1787 with the purification of the system of elections to Fellowships at Trinity, and at Oxford a systematic scheme of university examinations for a degree was instituted and enforced (the new school then instituted became the famous *Literae Humaniores*, the main basis of the work and fame of Oxford in the nineteenth century). Gladstone, Member of Parliament for Oxford University, helped sponsor the reforms at Oxford, and later, as Chancellor of the Exchequer, commissioned the Northcote-Trevelyan inquiry[16].

Later in the century pressure for reform was also exerted from outside – London University was founded in 1826 and it was particularly noticeable that after the 1832 Reform Bill the authorities at Oxford and Cambridge were surrounded by powerful critics and therefore had every incentive to put their house in order to prevent attack. For the first fifty years of the nineteenth century the universities were left alone by Parliament, but after 1850, the Royal Commission of Inquiry reporting in 1852 was followed by the Oxford Act of 1854 and the Cambridge Act of 1856; the Universities Tests Act of 1871 opened the universities to persons of all ways of thinking about religion, and the Royal Commission of 1872–4 on the financial resources of the Universities and Colleges, was followed by the Oxford and Cambridge Act of 1877 and the Legislation of the Statutory Commissions of 1877–82.

Before these reforms the situation in the universities was not untypical of eighteenth-century public institutions and it would be unjust to condemn the universities for their lethargy, corruption and sinecurism without remembering the conditions in the House of Commons, the Municipal Corporations, Government Offices, the Armed Services, or the Church: they were all more or less corrupt and lethargic.

At Oxford most of the Professors had ceased to lecture and were said to have given up even the pretence of teaching, sometimes from incompetence or laziness, but more often for want of an intellectual audience. The University had practically ceased to examine students before selling them even the B.A. degree. John Scott (later Lord Eldon) graduated in 1770 and by way of examination he was asked two questions to test him in Hebrew and History: 'What is the Hebrew for the place of a skull?' and 'Who founded University

College ?' By replying 'Golgotha' and 'King Alfred' he tells us that he satisfied the examiners who asked him nothing else.

But in 1822 Cambridge established the 'Previous Examination', designed to test the work of men in their second year, and in 1824 the Classical Tripos was set up.

In 1852 the Royal Commission on Oxford University reported that 'the Examinations have become the chief instrument not only for testing the proficiency of the students, but also for stimulating and directing the Studies of the place'. And in 1922 the Royal Commission on Oxford and Cambridge Universities reported that: 'The zeal and excitement aroused year after year in both Universities over the examinations for degrees put fresh life into the stagnant waters of Oxford and Cambridge, and gave to the system of competitive examination a prestige in the country at large which led to its adoption, not only as the fashionable panacea in all matters educational, but as the peculiarly British method of recruiting Civil Servants.'[17]

It is particularly interesting to notice the development of the School of *Literae Humaniores* – or 'Greats', as it is often called – at Oxford. Apart from its seniority and the fact that in the nineteenth century it outstripped the other Schools in numbers, it has been regarded as peculiarly characteristic of Oxford and a large number of able and distinguished Oxford men have passed through it. The philosophical side of the School includes Political Philosophy, Ethics, Logic and Metaphysics, and a considerable feeling of life was breathed into the School by the inspiring teaching of T. H. Green, to whose lectures large numbers of students would come anxious to learn the truth about the universe and human life[18] – these students included a significant proportion of men who later became senior Indian or Home civil servants and had the opportunity to put into practice aspects of the philosophy they had studied.[19]

Furthermore, in a number of respects the lives of these men resembled those of Plato's guardians whom they had studied. Plato envisaged a state ruled by guardians where the aim would be to secure the greatest possible happiness for the community as a whole. Plato taught that the guardians should not have private houses and were not to know their parents: this was slightly modified in nineteenth-century England so that when they were about eight years old the children from whom rulers were to be chosen were taken away from home for three-quarters of the year and taught not to mention their mothers or their own Christian names, but on the whole they were brought up in the traditions of the Sparta which Plato had advised.

Sir Charles Trevelyan (of the Northcote-Trevelyan Report) was Assistant Secretary at the Treasury[20] responsible for the radical proposals to reform his own and a number of other departments. He began his public service career with four terms at Haileybury where he won prizes, then spent a number of years in India. While in India Trevelyan met Macaulay and later married Macaulay's sister Hannah. As already mentioned, Macaulay discussed with his brother-in-law his proposals for reform of the Indian Civil Service before he put the final touches to his Report of 1854. Trevelyan was the original of Sir Gregory Hardlines in Anthony Trollope's *The Three Clerks*. Trollope later explained that in introducing the character of Sir Gregory Hardlines he 'intended to lean very heavily on that much-loathed scheme of competitive examination of which at that time Sir Charles Trevelyan was the great apostle'.[21]

Benjamin Jowett, the Master of Balliol, who exercised considerable influence on his contemporaries, was also a close friend of Macaulay (Geoffrey Faber relates that round about 1853 Jowett constantly visited Sir Charles Trevelyan's house in Westbourne Terrace where they would meet together with Macaulay).[22] Jowett had experience of the University reforms, particularly the changes in the examination system, and also happened to be in close touch with T. H. Green and the other Oxford Idealists. He had extreme views about what men can do by hard work and self-mastery and published a considerable amount of work on Plato. A caricature of Jowett appears in *The Three Clerks* in the person of Mr Jobbles.

Sir Stafford Northcote (the other half of the Northcote-Trevelyan team) went to Eton and also happened to be a Balliol undergraduate contemporary of Jowett (they were both awarded first class honours degrees in *Literae Humaniores* in 1839). Before being called to the bar he became W. E. Gladstone's Private Secretary at the Board of Trade. Gladstone recognised the interdependence of the three fields of reform: the Indian Civil Service, the Universities, and the Home Civil Service, and in a letter to Sir James Graham dated 1854, he said: 'In the case of Haileybury we struck an undisguised and deadly blow at patronage; in the case of Oxford we are likely to propose measures which I think are strong, but I hope will be salutary for the purpose of setting up competition as against restriction or private favour; I

am convinced that we have it in our power to render an immense
service to the country by a circumspect but energetic endeavour to
apply a like principle to the Civil Service and the great administrative
departments'.[23] Northcote also appears in *The Three Clerks* under the
name of Sir Warwick West End.

THE NORTHCOTE-TREVELYAN REPORT

There is a sense in which there was no Civil Service in Britain until
after the middle of the nineteenth century; there were many officials,
but they would not have regarded themselves as belonging to a
service. There were no common principles of recruitment, control,
or organization in the various departments of the central government.
1855 is generally taken as the beginning of the Civil Service as we
know it.[24]

Conditions of recruitment and service in government departments
before the middle of the nineteenth century have been well illustrated
in the writings of successful civil servants. Three examples are in
the published writings of Anthony Trollope, Edmund Yates and
Herbert Preston-Thomas.

Trollope, in his *Autobiography*, gives an interesting description
of how he was recruited to work in The General Post Office. He said,

'. . . a letter reached me, offering me a clerkship in the General
Post Office and I accepted it. Among my mother's dearest friends
she reckoned Mrs Freeling, the wife of Clayton Freeling, whose
father, Sir Francis Freeling, then ruled the Post Office. She had heard
of my desolate position, and had begged from her father-in-law the
offer of a berth in his own office.

'. . . I was asked to copy some lines from *The Times* newspaper
with an old quill pen, and at once made a series of blots and false
spellings. "That won't do, you know", said Henry Freeling to his
brother Clayton. Clayton, who was my friend, urged that I was
nervous, and asked that I might be allowed to do a bit of writing at
home and bring it as a sample on the next day. I was then asked
whether I was proficient at arithmetic. What could I say? I had
never learned the multiplication table, and had no more idea of the
rule of three than of conic sections. "I know a little of it", I said humbly,
whereupon I was sternly assured that on the morrow, should I succeed
in showing that my handwriting was all that it ought to be, I should

be examined as to that little of arithmetic. If that little should not be found to comprise a thorough knowledge of all the ordinary rules, together with practised and quick skill, my career in life could not be made at the Post Office. Going down the main stairs of the building – stairs which have I believe been now pulled down to make room for sorters and stampers – Clayton Freeling told me not to be too down-hearted. I was myself inclined to think that I had better at once go back to the school at Brussels. But nevertheless I went to work, and under the surveillance of my elder brother made a beautiful transcript of four or five pages of Gibbon. With a faltering heart I took this on the next day to the office. With my calligraphy I was contented, but was certain that I should come to the ground among the figures. But when I got to "The Grand", as we used to call our office in those days, from its site, St Martin's le Grand, I was seated at a desk without any further reference to my competency. No one condescended even to look at my beautiful penmanship.'[25]

Edmund Yates's account of how he joined the Post Office in 1847 illustrates by comparison with Trollope, the lack of uniformity in selection procedures. He said,

'. . . My godfather, Edmund Byng, had mentioned my appointment to two young fellows of his acquaintance who were in the office, and they speedily introduced themselves to me and set me at my ease. There was no examination in those days; I had not even to write from dictation, or do a rule-of-three sum, as had Anthony Trollope thirteen years before.'[26]

Another illustration of how the examination system worked in its early days is given by Herbert Preston-Thomas, who began his career in the Privy Council Office. He said,

'It was towards the end of the year 1859 that, fresh from Marlborough, I distinguished myself by gaining the first place in a competition held by the Civil Service Commissioners for a clerkship in the Privy Council Office. Frankness compels me to add that the two other nominees (required by the regulations to make up the prescribed number of three) may possibly have been the special couple known as the "Treasury Idiots", who could never pass anything, and were sent up again and again to give a walk-over to any Minister's protégé able to reach the standard of minimum qualifications. At any rate, they could barely read or write, and so I found myself entitled to a desk in Downing Street.'[27]

The Northcote-Trevelyan Report on the Organization of the Permanent Civil Service was an impressively concise paper of about twenty pages. However, it did not appear as the result of an isolated investigation but as the culmination of a series of inquiries into public offices in the 1840s and 1850s. Indeed, by 1854 reports had been produced on at least eleven departments. This 'finale' aspect of the report is important as there is a sense in which it is really the conclusion of all the reports together. This is seen in the opening sentence of the Report which says,

'We now proceed with that part of our instructions which states that, in connection with the inquiries which we were directed to make into each particular office, it is highly necessary that the conditions which are common to all the public establishments, such as the preliminary testimonials of character and bodily health to be required from candidates for public employment, the examination into their intellectual attainments, and the regulation of the promotions, should be carefully considered, so as to obtain full security for the public that none but qualified persons will be appointed, and that they will afterwards have every practical inducement to the active discharge of their duties.'

This sentence is in fact a word for word restatement of the terms of reference in the Treasury minute[28] appointing Northcote and Trevelyan to conduct the inquiry. Indeed, after considering the terms of reference and the nature of the report, Sir Kenneth Wheare has described it as 'a broadsheet, or broadside; it is a manifesto on Civil Service reform . . . a reformer's tract or pamphlet, unaccompanied by the usual apparatus of minutes of evidence, and the like.'[29]

It seems likely that, when writing their most famous report, Northcote and Trevelyan drew mainly on their personal experience and the evidence they had collected during the earlier investigations of various departments. There is a remarkable similarity in the wording of some of the recommendations in the earlier reports and the wording in the final report, and it is probably necessary to bear this in mind when considering the famous report itself. Some examples, taken from the earlier reports, will make this clear.[30]

On 3rd November 1848 a Treasury minute appointed W. Gibson Craig, J. Parker, and C. E. Trevelyan to inquire into 'the present state of the Establishment of the Treasury, and into the arrangements and regulations for the distribution and conduct of the business, in order

C

that such changes may be made as may be required to secure the highest practicable degree of efficiency'. The Report, dated 2nd March 1849, recommended 'that merit and qualification, and not seniority, should be the prevailing motives in selecting persons for promotion'. It also stated: 'We have no amendment to suggest in the existing rules which require that there should be an examination previously to admission, and a year's probation before the appointment is confirmed; and we recommend that they should be strictly acted upon, and that the superior officers of the Treasury should be enjoined, as well for the sake of the young men themselves, as on public grounds, to take immediate notice of any neglect of duty on the part of those serving under them.'

On 15th December 1849 Gibson Craig, Trevelyan and Herman Merivale submitted their report on the Colonial Office. They recommended that recruitment of Clerks should be 'conditional upon the candidate being not less than 20 and not more than 25 years of age, and upon its being shown, by the result of a suitable examination, that he is highly educated, and of unequivocal ability; and also to subject him to a year's probation after his admission.' They also recommended that 'promotion from class to class depend upon superior merit and qualification in a much greater degree than heretofore.'

On 20th March 1853, Trevelyan, Northcote and J. Booth submitted their report on the Board of Trade. They recommended 'that both the Clerks and the Copyists should undergo an examination previously to their appointment' and 'With regard to the examination of the Clerks, or superior class of Officers, we do not desire to lay down any very minute regulations: but we consider that it should be of such a nature as to show whether the candidate has had a liberal education, and whether he is personally intelligent'. They added 'we cannot avoid expressing our opinion, that the whole subject of the examination of candidates for public employment is well worthy of consideration, and that it would be of great advantage if a proper system were devised, and a central Board of properly qualified examiners appointed, without whose certificates no persons should be placed on the public establishments'.

On 25th May 1853 Trevelyan and Northcote submitted their report on the Department of Practical Science and Art.

On 20th June 1853 Courtenay, John Sadleir, Northcote and Trevelyan reported on the Poor Law Board. They wrote: 'We learn with satisfaction that the rule of regulating promotion by a strict reference to merit, which ought never to be lost sight of in any Government Department, has been carefully observed in this Office. . . . We are of the opinion that . . . both the Clerks and the Supplementary Clerks should be examined previously to their appointment. . . . The candidates for clerkships of the superior class should be examined with a view to ascertain that they have received a liberal education, and are personally intelligent. . . . The age of admission to clerkships should be between eighteen and twenty-five years; and none should be eligible beyond those limits'.

On the 6th August 1853 C. C. Greville, Trevelyan and Northcote reported on the Privy Council Office. They said: 'With regard to the future selection of gentlemen to fill the office of Second Clerk, we are of opinion that it would be desirable to require the candidate to pass an examination for the purpose of ascertaining that he has received a liberal education, and that he is personally intelligent. We do not desire to lay down any precise rules as to the nature of such examination; it should, to a certain extent, depend upon that of the candidate's previous studies; but care should be taken to ascertain that he is a person of sufficient capacity and attainments to justify the expectation that he will in due time be fit to be promoted to the appointment of First Clerk. . . . The promotion of the Clerks from class to class, and the selection of gentlemen to fill the Offices of Secretary or Assistant Secretary, should be strictly according to merit.'

On 10th August 1853 T. W. C. Murdock, Trevelyan and Northcote reported on the Colonial Land and Emigration Office. 'The candidates for clerkships of the superior class should further be examined with a view to ascertain that they have received a liberal education, and are personally intelligent . . . the nature of this examination . . . may . . . to a certain extent, be made to depend upon the nature of the candidate's previous studies.'

On 17th December 1853 Northcote, Trevelyan, W. G. Anderson and E. A. Hoffay reported on the Board of Ordnance. They recommended examinations before appointments and that the nature of the examination should depend on 'the previous studies of those who come before them as candidates. They should be so conducted as to ascertain that the person examined is intelligent, and that he had received a liberal education'.

On 14th January 1854 Northcote and Trevelyan reported on the Office of Works.

On 30th May 1854 Elcho, Northcote, Trevelyan and Hoffay reported on the Post Office.

All these reports, previous to the more general one on the Organization of the Civil Service, provided an opportunity for trying out the most important ideas that were to be contained in the final report. In effect, they constituted a splendid series of pilot studies.

The famous Northcote-Trevelyan Report has been reprinted a number of times, including in *Public Administration* (the Journal of the Royal Institute of Public Administration) in 1954, and as an appendix to the Report of the Fulton Committee.[31] The following is a summary of the main features of the Report.

The objects of the recommendations were:

'1. To provide, by a proper system of examination, for the supply of the public with a thoroughly efficient class of men.

2. To encourage industry and foster merit, by teaching all public servants to look forward to promotion according to their deserts, and to expect the highest prizes in the Service if they can qualify themselves for them.

3. To mitigate the evils which result from the fragmentary character of the Service, and to introduce into it some elements of unity, by placing the first appointments upon a uniform footing, opening the way to the promotion of public officers to staff appointments in other departments than their own, and introducing into the lower ranks a body of men (the supplementary clerks) whose services may be made available at any time in any office whatever.'

The Report said that the Civil Service did not attract the ablest men, but instead it was sought after by the unambitious, indolent or incapable. This was because the work was comparatively light and there was provision for retirement in the event of bodily incapacity. The result was that the Service suffered both in internal efficiency and in public estimation. The effects of the patronage system meant that the best men were not chosen for office (though in many offices some kind of examination system operated) and even when able men were appointed nothing was done to make the best use of their talents. And since it was a fragmentary Service, promotions were made only within departments.

It suggested that the best method of getting good civil servants, and of making the most of them after they were recruited, was to train young men carefully selected by examination and whose permanent appointment would be confirmed only after the satisfactory completion of a short period of probation. In order to ensure that the examinations would be carried out in an effective and consistent manner throughout the Service, the Report recommended that a Central Board of Examiners should be established, and the examination should be a competitive literary examination (plus an inquiry into the age, health and moral fitness of the candidates). There should be a proper distinction between intellectual and mechanical work and for the intellectual positions the examination should contain an extensive range of subjects and should be open to all persons of a given age and on a level with 'the highest description of education in this country'; there should be a lower standard to test for the more 'mechanical' clerkships.

Once in the Service, the recruit should be transferred from one department of the office to another so that he would be given the opportunity of making himself master of the whole of the department's business, then his promotion should depend on merit and not on seniority.

Appended to the Report, and published with it, was a letter from Jowett in which he outlined a scheme of four 'schools' or subjects for examination, and the desirability of holding the examinations throughout the country.

Gladstone, who commissioned the Northcote-Trevelyan inquiry, conceived its task as 'to draw up a general Report on the state of the Civil Service with a statement of remedies broader and larger in their nature than could conveniently be treated of in the separate reports of each distinct establishment'.[32] Before the Report was presented to Parliament a number of leading educationalists in the country were invited by Trevelyan to state their opinions on it. They agreed that the plan would 'give a powerful impulse to the education of all classes', but none recognised more clearly than Gladstone that a competitive examination with classics and mathematics as 'staple' subjects would play straight into the hands of the great public schools and colleges. In January 1854 Gladstone wrote to Lord John Russell:

'I do not hesitate to say that one of the great recommendations

of the change in my eyes would be its tendency to strengthen and
multiply the ties between the higher classes and the possession of
administrative power. As a member for Oxford, I look forward eagerly
to its operation. There, happily, we are not without some lights of
experience to throw upon this part of the subject. The objection which
I always hear there from persons who wish to retain restrictions
upon elections is this: "If you leave them to examination, Eton,
Harrow, Rugby and the other public schools will carry *everything*".
I have a strong impression that the aristocracy of this country are
even superior in natural gifts, on the average, to the mass: but it is
plain that with their acquired advantages, their *insensible* education,
irrespective of book learning, they have an immense superiority.
This applies in its degree to all those who may be called gentlemen
by birth and training; and it must be remembered that an essential
part of any such plan as is now under discussion is the separation
of *work*, whenever it can be made, into mechanical and intellectual,
a separation which will open to the highly educated class a career and
give them a command over all the higher parts of the civil service,
which up to this time they have never enjoyed'.[33]

From the outset some commentators recognised that the plan was
never intended to afford equal opportunities to all social classes.
Sir Francis Baring, the distinguished financier and public servant,
doubted whether 'the practical operation of their much-vaunted
competitive system, which was to be open to all the world, would not
ultimately be to throw all the best appointments in the public service
into the hands of the richer portion of the community'. But on the
other hand, it is also known that Queen Victoria had grave misgivings
lest competitive examinations would fill the public offices with 'low
people without breeding or feelings of gentlemen'.

After the publication of the Report there were public discussions
in print and a number of eminent civil servants and others sprang to
the defence of the Service, maintaining that the charges in the Report
were unjust and without foundation. Edwin Chadwick, one of the
defenders, declared that: 'All who are acquainted with the narrow
circle of the highest class of permanent officers in the Civil Service,
will speak of them with respect; and for myself, I should testify
that most of them are in nowise exceeded in business, power and
devotion, and are rarely equalled in general capacity and accomplishments by the chiefs of the highest manufacturing, commercial and

mercantile establishments which lead the prosperity of the empire.'

On the other hand, there was also an impressive array of defendants of the Report including John Stuart Mill, who believed that the adoption of competitive examinations would form an era in history. Macaulay noted in his journal: 'There was open-mouthed criticism of the Report at Brooks'. Trevelyan has been too sanguine; the pear is not ripe. I always thought so. The time will come but it is not come yet.'

SINCE THE NORTHCOTE-TREVELYAN REPORT

In January 1854 the Queen's speech at the opening of Parliament had declared the government's intention of effecting a reform in the Civil Service, although at that time the Northcote-Trevelyan Report had not been presented to Parliament. The Report was eventually presented on 24th January, but Parliament then heard no more about administrative reform until the Civil Service Commission was set up by Order in Council on 21st May 1855, by which time there was widespread agitation for reform because of mismanagement of the Crimean War.

Public agitation about the conduct of the War had been aroused by the dispatches from the Crimea of W. H. Russell, war correspondent of *The Times*, and his accounts of the sufferings of British troops there were supported from other sources. There were debates in Parliament and at the beginning of 1855 a Select Committee of Inquiry was established 'to inquire into the conduct of our army before Sebastopol, and into the conduct of those departments of the Government whose duty it has been to minister to the wants of the army'. The report of the Committee was published in June 1855 and constituted a severe indictment of the administrative chaos which it found. The report concluded:

'Your Committee report that the sufferings of the army resulted mainly from the circumstances under which the expedition to the Crimea was undertaken and executed. The administration which ordered that expedition had no adequate information as to the amount of forces in the Crimea. They were not acquainted with the strength of the fortress to be attacked or with the resources of the country to be invaded. They hoped and expected the expedition to be immediately successful; and as they did not foresee the probability of a protracted struggle, they made no provision for a winter campaign. The patience and fortitude of the army demand the admiration of the nation on whose behalf they have fought, bled and suffered. Their heroic valour, and equally heroic patience under sufferings and privations, have given them claims on the country which will doubtless be gratefully acknowledged. Your Committee will now close their report with a hope that every British army may in future display the valour which this noble army has displayed, and that none may hereafter be exposed to such sufferings as have been recorded in these pages.'[34]

Mismanagement of the Crimean War thus caused considerable public concern, and led to the publication of a number of pamphlets and leading articles in newspapers and journals at the time. For example, an article entitled 'Administrative Reform – The Civil Service' in *Blackwood's Magazine* (1855) began: 'Though war is in itself a great and grievous calamity, it by no means follows as a necessary consequence that its effects may not be, in various ways, beneficial to the nation which has been compelled in a just cause to draw the sword.'[35] And a pamphlet entitled *Our Government Offices*, published in 1855, stated: 'In the following pages a plan is suggested with the object of making the Civil Service immediately useful in the organization of the war, and permanently efficient as a working element of the State . . . Our reform must be immediate, for war will not wait – and we have no time to train up a new class of clerks . . . The army supplies an illustration of the change that is necessary; officers have rank "in the army", distinct from their *regimental* rank. In the same way officers in the Civil Service should be classified according to their rank in the whole Service, distinct from their *"departmental"* rank. It matters little what names are given to the different ranks of the Service, although the term "clerk" might be altered with advantage, making it more analogous to the Civil Service of India, which stands so high.'[36]

The Northcote-Trevelyan Report had envisaged its suggested reforms being embodied in an Act of Parliament but the Government decided otherwise. Instead, an Order in Council was made and Sir George Cornewall Lewis, who supported the procedure, argued that the setting up of a board of examiners 'would necessarily entail some expense, and however small this might be, it would necessitate an annual vote which would give the House of Commons a practical veto upon the system once in every session'. Consequently, there was no full dress debate in Parliament on the reforms as they were introduced: indeed, the first debate on the subject did not take place until three weeks after the Order in Council was made.

The Order in Council on 21st May set up a Civil Service Commission with Sir Edward Ryan (a friend of Macaulay, and ex-Chief Justice of Bengal) as Chairman, and the other two members were Mr Shaw Lefevre (Clerk to the House of Lords), and Mr Edward Romilly (Chairman of the Audit Board). It was empowered to arrange with the responsible heads of the various departments the conditions of entry into their respective departments; decisions on examination subjects, age limits and other such conditions were in fact left to the departmental chiefs. Professor Edward Hughes has explained: 'The Civil Service Commissioners had to examine such candidates, and such candidates only, as had been nominated or placed on probation by the head of the department since 21st May, they were to see that candidates conformed to the particular conditions laid down—i.e. their essential function was authentication. It was, of course, open to any head of department to arrange with the Civil Service Commissioners that a limited number of candidates should compete for each vacancy, so that no single candidate should have a walk-over. This was a system which Palmerston himself favoured and, in fact, this is what Labouchère, Secretary of State for the Colonies, did from the first. By contrast, the Civil Service Commissioners themselves made admissions to clerkships in their own office conditional upon success in an open competition, and the Home Office and Board of Works followed suit in 1857. But most departments clung to "limited competition" among a selected number of nominated candidates. It was even said that Hayter, the Secretary of the Treasury, still nominated "at his pleasure" some 240 clerks a year in the revenue services. Only in 1857 did the government declare that the principle of "limited" competition was to obtain in all departments dependent on the Treasury.'[37]

In 1857 the House of Commons recorded its unanimous opinion that the experience acquired since the issuing of the Order in Council of May 21st 1855, was in favour of the adoption of the principle of competition as a condition of entrance to the Civil Service.

In February 1860 the House of Commons appointed a Select Committee 'to inquire into the present mode of nominating and examining candidates for junior appointments in the Civil Service with a view to ascertaining whether greater facility may not be afforded for the admission of properly qualified persons'. In July 1860 the Committee reported that while the Order in Council of 1855 had checked some of the abuses that had previously existed it had for the most part been evaded; the competitions held under it had for the most part been shams and 'a fertile source of abuse'; and finally that the large percentage of rejections on the ground of unfitness, educational, physical and moral, proved how wanting the nominating authorities had been in the sense of responsibility. The Committee insisted on a real and effective system of competition, in place of the sham competition they found in existence, with open competition as the next step.

Although the Civil Service Commission was established in 1855 and the abolition of patronage had been recommended by Northcote and Trevelyan, patronage had not, in fact, been abolished. A check had been placed upon its misuse, but there were still elements of it left, and Sir Stanley Leathes has related a story that long ago when the Commissioners refused to sign a certificate in favour of a certain person, the Prime Minister appointed an extra commissioner (unpaid) who signed the certificate and never appeared again in the office.[38]

However, devices for preserving opportunities for patronage within the form of impartiality were largely swept away by the Order in Council of 4th June 1870, which, with certain exceptions, made open competition obligatory throughout the Home Civil Service. Also, before that time, the power of the Civil Service Commission had been strengthened in 1859 when the Superannuation Act of that year enacted that no civil servant should receive a pension unless he possessed a certificate of competency from the Civil Service Commission.

Since the Northcote-Trevelyan Report there have been six further major inquiries.

In 1874 the Playfair Committee (not a Royal Commission, but a Departmental Committee, whose chairman was Sir Lyon Playfair) emphasised the distinction between routine and intellectual work and recommended a greater division of labour and differentiation of functions, together with the specialised recruitment of men to correspond to this differentiation. The Lower Division (consisting of the

'Playfair' Clerks, as they were first called) owed its development to the Playfair Report, which originated the plan of having a class of general clerks who could easily be transferred from one office to another. The Report recommended that the Higher Division should be a small body recruited from men between the ages of 18 and 23, who had received a public school or university education, and the Lower Division should be recruited from men between the ages of 17 and 20 who had received an ordinary commercial education. As the majority of members of the Playfair Committee were civil servants (six of its eight members were Heads of Departments), it had the appearance of a professional body taking evidence mainly from those concerned with the day-to-day work of the Civil Service.

But most of the Playfair recommendations came to nothing. The Order in Council of 12th February 1876 purported to deal with the recommendations of the Committee, but in fact it only dealt with the recommendations affecting the Lower Division (Clerks and Boy Clerks), and referred to the Higher Division only indirectly in connection with promotion into it from the Lower Division. In general, the Report did little more than build upon the foundation laid by the recommendations of Northcote and Trevelyan. It emphasised the importance of open competitive examinations, and as far as recruitment was concerned, stressed the need for uniformity as the Service was still organized on a departmental basis.

Then in 1886 the Ridley Commission reported and confirmed the general principles laid down by the Playfair Committee. It considered the division of work in the Service between the Higher Division and the Lower Division – it found that Higher Division men were filling positions which could equally well be held by men in the Lower Division and this was expensive as well as leading to discontent in the Service. As a result of the recommendations of the Ridley Commission rigid departmentalism was broken down as far as the Second Division was concerned by the end of the nineteenth century, but it remained a distinctive characteristic of the First Division (as it was called after 1890) until well into the twentieth century.

Next came the Royal Commission appointed in 1912 under the chairmanship of Lord MacDonnell and which reported in 1914. It was required to report on existing methods of making appointments to the Civil Service, on the working of the open competitive examination system, and to recommend alterations and improvements. The

Commissioners found that there were still seven methods of appointment to the Service, and they censured the remaining opportunities for patronage. The MacDonnell recommendations influenced the reconstruction schemes which were being put forward to enable the Service to recover from the abnormal war conditions and to adjust to contemporary needs (for example, it recommended the competitive interview as a method for recruiting professional officers, a form of selection which has become more sophisticated since, and the Mac-Donnell recommendations in that respect may be regarded as a prelude to what has now become the only method of direct entry recruitment by open competition to the Assistant Principal grade).

In 1918, a committee[39], appointed to consider the Class I examinations for the Civil Service, noted the difficulty in assigning an order of merit to candidates examined in various combinations of subjects. Whilst there was no question of abandoning the examination system, still recognised as the most objective method of assessing merit so far devised, modifications were recommended. Consequently, after the First World War oral examinations were used to supplement the written examination, though there were doubts about what the interviews were supposed to test, and also about possible bias in the examiners.

In 1929 the Tomlin Royal Commission was appointed and heard arguments for and against the examination system. Evidence showed that the system not only favoured the older universities at the expense of the younger, but also those whose preliminary education had been carried on in the kind of schools which provided a good grounding in classical languages. The Commission, which reported in 1931, recommended the retention of the interview but said that care should be exercised in the selection of the personnel of interviewing boards.

The Priestley Royal Commission which reported in 1955 made a number of recommendations on superannuation, hours of work, leave, etc., mainly on the basis of what is known as the principle of fair comparison (that is, comparing conditions in the Civil Service with similar positions outside the Service). There were no changes in the Service of fundamental significance following the report; leave was cut for new entrants and the Civil Service Pay Research Unit was established.

The Fulton Committee reported in 1968.[40] It said that the 'Home

Civil Service today is still fundamentally the product of the nineteenth-century philosophy of the Northcote-Trevelyan Report. The tasks it faces are those of the second half of the twentieth century. This is what we have found; it is what we seek to remedy.' Its main recommendations were to do away with the cult of the all-rounder and make the Service more professional by making more specialist the members of the general classes and more management-conscious the members of the specialist classes. In addition, it recommended the abolition of the class structure, which it said should be replaced by a single grading structure in which there are an appropriate number of pay-levels matching different levels of skill and responsibility. It also made a number of recommendations to make the Service more aware of management processes (particularly personnel management) including the setting up of a Civil Service Department to take over the work previously performed by both the Pay and Management group of divisions of the Treasury and the Civil Service Commission.

SUMMARY

The Northcote-Trevelyan Report is important for two reasons. First, it marks the beginning of the modern Civil Service in Britain. Before 1854 there had been a number of government officials working in a number of departments each of which had its own separate organization, recruitment procedures and methods of working. There was no unity; there were officials but there was not a Service. There had been inquiries and reports into various government departments but Northcote and Trevelyan were the first to consider 'the conditions which are common to all the public establishments'.

Secondly, the Northcote-Trevelyan Report laid down three principles which have since been generally accepted and adopted. There is now a proper system of recruitment by examination, promotion based on industry and merit (with an element of seniority), and other common features which have fostered unity in the Civil Service. These fundamental principles were recommended in 1854 and introduced in stages in the following century. Other inquiries and reports in the next hundred years have done little more than re-emphasise the general principles and recommend how they might best be implemented in the circumstances then existing. A survey of the inquiries from 1854 to 1955 reveals a gradual process of consolidation and adaptation.

Other influences have also been significant. The reforms in the Indian Civil Service provided a useful pilot study for the introduction of reforms into the Home Civil Service. The new emphasis on examinations and other reforms in Oxford and Cambridge Universities and the establishment of London University were also relevant. But important as they were, they could have been equally relevant for reforms in other non-public institutions. There had to be another essential ingredient, a political ingredient, for the particular reforms in public administration.

The political ingredient was primarily supplied by public reactions to the conduct of the Crimean War. The relative party positions and attitudes in Parliament also helped, for after the Reform Act there was an enthusiasm for reforms outside Parliament as well. But such feeling in Parliament was not as important as the disclosures about mismanagement in the Crimea and it was those disclosures which focused political attention on the need for reform in the Civil Service.

3. Recruitment

'The real "Second Chamber", the real "constitutional check" in England, is provided, not by the House of Lords or the Monarchy, but by the existence of a permanent Civil Service, appointed on a system independent of the opinion or desires of any politician and holding office during good behaviour.'[1]

In the previous chapter an attempt was made to provide a historical sketch of the most important stages in the development of the higher Civil Service. This chapter is concerned with recruitment and in it emphasis will be given to what may be called the principles of recruitment and how these principles are applied in the systems of recruitment operating at the present time.

PRINCIPLES OF RECRUITMENT

What makes the Northcote-Trevelyan Report so important today is that the principles of recruitment which it laid down are still applied and with modifications constitute the basis of the present methods of selection.

Before the middle of the last century – indeed, up to 1870 – the method of recruitment was quite simple: patronage. Although the first step away from patronage as a system of recruitment was taken when the Civil Service Commission was established in 1855, it was not until 1870 that it was politically and administratively opportune to formally get rid of the patronage system. The passing of the Superannuation Act of 1859, which enacted that, with certain minor exceptions, no civil servant should receive a pension unless he possessed a certificate of competency from the Civil Service Commission, had greatly strengthened the position of that body and of those who wished to extend its power. So it was in 1870 that the Treasury issued the famous Order in Council which both formally abolished patronage and established the system of Open Competition.

Faced with difficulties in attracting really able men into the Civil Service, the Northcote-Trevelyan Report made recommendations for selection which can be summarised in two general principles. First, they should attract the ablest men by a competitive examination open to all classes of the population, conducted by an independent central board. Secondly, for the superior positions, efforts should be made to secure the services of the most promising young men of the day by an examination on a level with the highest standards of education in the country.

The overriding principle recommended in the 1854 Report on the Indian Civil Service[2] was that the method of selection should be suited to the education system of the country. As the Report stated: 'The youth who does best what all the ablest and most ambitious youths about him are trying to do well will generally prove a superior man'. Furthermore, it was thought that a fair intellectual test on such a basis would also serve another purpose, for 'early superiority in science and literature generally indicates the existence of some qualities which are securities against vice – industry, self-denial, a taste for pleasures not sensual, a laudable desire of honourable distinction, a still more laudable desire to obtain the approbation of friends and relations. We therefore believe that the intellectual test which is about to be established will be found in practice to be also the best test that can be devised'.

As far as the details were concerned, the Report recommended that the whole examination should be carried on by means of written papers. The subjects were not to be narrowly relevant to the India situation, indeed it was specifically stated that other subjects should not be neglected to enable candidates to specialise in Indian subjects. In addition, 'the examination should be of such a nature that no candidate who may fail should, to whatever calling he may betake himself, have any reason to regret the time and labour which he spent in preparing himself to be examined'.

The subjects of the examination were therefore to give candidates the greatest possible scope in their studies – though they were, of course, to be based on the subjects taught in universities at that time. Subjects specifically mentioned in the Report included English history and literature, Greek, Latin, French, German, Italian, Mathematics (pure and mixed), Natural Sciences (Chemistry, Geology, Mineralogy, Botany, Zoology), Moral Sciences (Moral and Political

Philosophy), Sanscrit and Arabic. As for the marking system, this was to be arranged so that 'no part of the kingdom, and no class of schools, shall exclusively furnish servants to the East India Company'.

The Committee recognised that there was also specialised knowledge which an Indian Civil Servant should obtain, and they recommended that the proper time to study relevant subjects was during the one or two year probationary period. Subjects they had in mind were government, law, financial and commercial science, and vernacular languages.

The consequences of this system of selection were not hidden from those making the recommendations or concerned with their implementation. Nor has it been hidden from observers reviewing the situation at later dates. As Robert Moses observed in 1914:

'Macaulay knew the public to whom he was opening the examinations; he knew perfectly well that open competition did not involve attracting the ill-bred and ill-balanced middle class into the Indian Service. Macaulay meant to open the competition to undergraduates of the great universities, and he expected that in an open competition with a high standard based on the Oxford and Cambridge honour schools, Oxford and Cambridge would more than hold their own. The scheme was not quite as democratic as it looked. Like the English cabinet and the English aristocracy, the Indian Civil Service was to be opened to gentlemen who had inherited breeding and culture, and to those of the middle class who had made themselves gentlemen by acquiring the same breeding and culture.'[3]

By 1908 the system was firmly in operation, so much so that criticisms all too familiar to those concerned with Civil Service selection in the twentieth-century were already being made. Lawrence Lowell, in *The Government of England*, wrote:

'As a matter of fact the papers in mathematics and natural science are based upon the requirements for honour degrees at Cambridge, the papers in classical and other subjects upon those at Oxford; and thus it happens that by far the larger part of the successful candidates come from one or other of these two great universities.'[4]

Lowell noted that of the 514 successful candidates for the Class I clerkships, the Indian Civil Service and the Eastern Cadets, from 1896 to 1900 inclusive, 262 had studied at Oxford, 148 at Cambridge, 83 at other universities in the United Kingdom, 7 in colonial and Indian universities, and 14 in no university at all.[5] Lowell's general comment on the whole situation was that 'it has come about that competitive

D

examination, instead of having a levelling tendency, by throwing
the Service open to a crowd of quick-witted youths without breeding,
has helped to strengthen the hold of the upper classes upon the
government, by reserving the most important posts for men trained
in the old aristocratic seats of learning'.[6]

The general principles had therefore been established in the nineteenth century. The general method of recruitment was to be by
open competitive examination and that competition was to be on a
level with the highest standards of education in the country. This
appeared very fair in theory; it was in practice that the system was
rather less impartial, for much depended on what was meant by 'the
highest standards of education in the country'.

The MacDonnell Royal Commission in 1912 soon found that the
examination system then in operation for admission to the First
Division was more favourable to candidates from Oxford and Cambridge than to those educated at smaller and newer universities.
Stanley M. Leathes, First Civil Service Commissioner, admitted:
'There is no doubt that it works out so . . .'[7] and later explained:
'Manchester in the last five years has only produced two successful
candidates, Leeds only one, and Birmingham does not appear to have
produced any . . . I imagine that these modern universities are very
largely concerned with professional training, training people for
particular professions (I believe they have a professor of brewing at
Birmingham, for instance), and that people do not go so much to the
new universities in order to get a considerable all-round education,
but rather to be prepared for a certain profession'.[8]

Leathes gave to the Commission recruitment figures for the period
1906–1910 inclusive in the combined competition for Class I Clerkships
in the Home Civil Service, Indian Civil Service, and Eastern Cadet-
ships. In those years there were 473 successful candidates and the
universities to which they belonged were:

Oxford	247	Glasgow	7
Cambridge	142	Aberdeen	6
Dublin	23	London	5
Edinburgh	17	Manchester	2
Royal University		Leeds	1
of Ireland	14	No university	9

Later, the Commission learned that in 1911, in the examination for the Home, Indian and Civil Service, out of the first 24 men, 16 had a classical education at either Oxford or Cambridge.[9]

They heard a number of complaints from representatives of provincial universities. For example, Sir Hiram Wilkinson, representing the University of Belfast, told the Commission that under the present syllabus, Belfast men competed 'at an enormous disadvantage with Oxford and Cambridge'. He also commented that the universities paid no regard to the Civil Service examinations and the Civil Service examinations had no regard for the curriculum of the universities. Consequently, the Civil Service Commissioners could not be expected to glean the best results of university training.[10]

Professor W. M. Hicks, Acting Vice-Chancellor of Sheffield University, told the MacDonnell Commission that the University of Sheffield had sent no students at all to the Class I examination of the Civil Service. He explained that most of their ablest students had a view to going into business connected with the City. However, he agreed that a student who might be reading for an honours degree in the University of Sheffield would be able to get only a very small number of marks in the Class I examination – though if he had the Civil Service examination in mind when he entered the university he could have chosen subjects accordingly and thereby increased his chances.[11]

Professor J. Wertheimer, of Bristol University, similarly complained about the examination syllabus – in particular because it laid excessive weight upon classics and classical subjects. He also said:

'. . . I am not by any means certain that it is altogether wise that these men should be chosen as they are at present, practically immediately after they have left the university and before they have had any outside experience of life. I am inclined to think that it tends somewhat – with respect to the Civil Service, many members of which I know and whose friendship I value – to make a class of "mandarins" who have not had sufficient experience of the outside world; and in some cases I think it leads to a certain amount of want of touch between the public and the high officials of the Civil Service'.[12]

There was little doubt that the system produced more recruits from Oxford and Cambridge than from elsewhere, the figures showed this, and the MacDonnell Report commented: '. . . the most salient fact emerging from an analysis of the academic antecedents of the successful candidates is the great numerical preponderance of those who have been educated at Oxford and Cambridge, especially Oxford.'[13] One witness boldly told the Commission of somebody who was at the London School of Economics and who felt that his education did not admit of his entering the examination as there was no correlation between the subjects he was studying and the syllabus for the Civil Service examinations. One of the Commissioners pointed out that it was possible for such a student to have chosen subjects given in the list for the Civil Service examination[14] – but no research was done to discover whether or not students arrived at the universities already determined on their careers. It seems to have been assumed by at least some members of the Commission, that, like Plato's guardians, top civil servants were born to their specific function.

It was not really denied that there was a bias towards Oxford and Cambridge and towards a classical education, though there were attempts to justify it. Dr J. R. Tanner of Oxford University, told the Commission that he thought the best kind of education was a combination of classics and history and he thought that combination produced the very best men.[15] Viscount Haldane explained:

'. . . experience has shown – at least, I think so – that, on the whole, classics are rather the best all-round training. I do not put it very high, and I do not call myself a classical scholar; it is not on those lines that my work has lain, but I have observed at the Bar, which is a very good place to observe it, that for a really all-round training a literary training, and particularly a Latin and Greek training, although it has its defects, and is by no means perfect, is a very good foundation, and it is probably that which has led to the large amounts being assigned to Latin and Greek here.'[16]

It was almost generally assumed that the highest standards must be at Oxford and Cambridge and that graduates of those universities (particularly in classics – the enthusiasts for Latin and Greek carried their arguments far beyond the point where Macaulay would have agreed with them) were 'best' without any adequate investigation being made of 'best' for what, beyond assuming that it was for non-routine or intellectual work. Knowledge of what higher civil servants did was generally assumed, but no investigation was made to find out what civil servants actually did. 'Best' was, in effect, a combination of playing safe in meeting a number of qualities connected with intellectual development together with a considerable element of 'establishment' prejudice.

An examination of the Minutes of Evidence before the MacDonnell Commission suggests the existence of a further principle in practice. It was that the Service required entrants with the highest quality yet widest possible general education and this meant that the specialist should be at a disadvantage. In fact, the candidate at most disadvantage was the one who had received instruction at practically every university in England except Oxford, and at Oxford the person who had received instruction under any other course than that of the Oxford Greats.[17]

Superficially, the concerns of the MacDonnell Royal Commission may now appear dated, but this is not really so. The subjects from which Civil Service candidates might choose to be examined were still controversial in the 1950s and 1960s. It was not until 1961 that the first paper in sociology was set. This may appear surprising as the subject had been taught for many years at the London School of Economics and at some provincial universities, but the first lecturer in sociology was not appointed to Cambridge University until 1959 and to Oxford University in 1962. One of the unsuccessful candidates in 1951, a London graduate in history, recently suggested to J. F. Pickering[18] that the group of history papers was still at that time slanted more in favour of the 'Oxbridge' historian than the 'Redbrick' candidate – he referred to the existence of questions on the history of art, music and literature to the exclusion of questions on social and economic history, questions which the Redbrick candidate was more likely to be able to answer. And as recently as 1969, in the last 'Method I' open competition, a student of sociology – one of the university subjects now in greatest demand by undergraduates – was at a distinct disadvantage when compared with, for example, a student of history, law, classics, French, German or one of the pure sciences (there were two papers on sociology worth a total of 200 marks; but eighteen papers on history worth 1800 marks, seventeen on law worth 1700 marks, ten on classics worth 1000 marks, six on French worth 700 marks, and six on German worth 700 marks).[19]

However, it should be remembered that the Method I competition no longer operates, and of the Method II competition the Davies committee was able to report in 1969 that 'Witnesses from the staffs of universities were confident that Method II was accepted as thorough and fair by the greatest majority of candidates'.[20] It added its own unanimous opinion: 'Having considered all the evidence ... Method II, and particularly c.s.s.b. [Civil Service Selection Board], is something to which the Public Service can point with pride.'[21]

METHODS OF RECRUITMENT

Whilst the principles of recruitment originate from recommendations made in the last century for the Home and Indian Civil Services, in practice there have been a number of modifications since those reports were published.

The traditional method of selection by written examination, for long the sole method of recruitment, meant that candidates for the Administrative Class took an examination in optional academic subjects at honours degree level. When an additional method of selection was introduced after the Second World War, the traditional procedure was referred to as Method I and the new procedure as Method II. The number of papers for Method I had continuously to be expanded because of the wide variations in the content of first degree courses and the growth of new specialisms, and as the pressures already referred to against bias at the beginning of the century were maintained and even increased by the 1950s and 1960s, the Civil Service Commission made efforts to meet some of the most obvious criticisms. By 1966 there were over 150 papers in the examination (though the Civil Service Commission told the Fulton Committee that it regarded the syllabus in many subjects as unsatisfactory) but there were only 63 candidates in that year. In 1968 there were 128 successful for the Administrative Class and Diplomatic Service by Method II but only 8 by Method I.[22] It is therefore not surprising that Method I has been discontinued; the last examination for it was held in 1969.

Recruitment by open competition to the Assistant Principal grade is therefore no longer by two methods. It is now only by what was previously known as 'Method II'. This consists of a qualifying examination in general subjects, followed by tests and interviews lasting two days at the Civil Service Selection Board, and an interview before the Final Selection Board. There are three such competitions a year. To be appointed under this method a candidate, except for those from the Forces and Overseas Civil Service, must normally have or obtain a first or second class honours degree and be under 28 years of age. Candidates with first class honours degrees or second class honours plus post-graduate degrees, may apply at any time and are exempt from the qualifying examination.

The qualifications for direct entry into the higher grades is somewhat more complex, though it follows a similar pattern. In general the age limit is higher and though no formal academic qualifications are necessary, the intellectual standard required is that of a good honours degree plus experience of administrative work.

At present there are, however, five methods of entry into the Administrative Class. These methods, as explained to the Fulton Committee[23] are:

1. By open competition to the Assistant Principal grade;

2. In order to introduce outside experience a competition for direct entry Principals between the ages of 30–35 was instituted in 1964. Up to the end of 1966, 31 Principals had been recruited under this scheme;

3. To meet shortages and assist resettlement, some recruitment direct to the Principal grade has taken place from candidates who are serving or former members of the Forces and Overseas Civil Service. In 1961, and again in 1965 and in 1966, this competition was thrown open to other candidates. The yield from the 1965 competition was about 50, and from the 1966 competition it was 40.

4. At the same time as direct recruitment of Principals at (2) was instituted, recruitment of up to three Assistant Secretaries a year was begun. Five appointments had been made up to 1968, and further competitions were being planned.

5. Entry from other classes is by:

(a) Limited competition to Assistant Principal grade. One-fifth of Assistant Principal vacancies to be filled are in theory reserved for entrants by this method, but the number of candidates of the required standard has not reached this proportion in recent years.

(b) Departmental and central transfer or promotion to Principal grade from outside the Administrative Class.

(c) In 1963 a scheme was started for trying out selected Executive Officers on Assistant Principal work. Those who showed promise were put through the Civil Service Selection Board at the end of the trial period and then interviewed by a departmental board with Civil Service Commission representation for promotion to Assistant Principal. This pilot scheme produced eight Assistant Principals. The exercise has been repeated in subsequent years.

(d) In 1964 a special exercise was carried out for members of the Scientific Officer Class who wished to be considered for transfer to the Administrative Class at Principal level; 13 candidates were then successful and the exercise has been repeated in subsequent years.

In practice, it is now usual to recruit less than a third of Administrative Class civil servants as direct entrants from universities through open competitions to the Assistant Principal grade. This is illustrated by the following information about entrants since 1960 to the Principal grade:

TABLE VII

NUMBERS OF ENTRANTS TO THE PRINCIPAL GRADE
IN RECENT YEARS, SHOWING SOURCE OF ENTRY[24]

Source of entry	1960	1961	1962	1963	1964	1965	1966
Assistant Principal, open competition entrant	34	33	40	31	37	43	44
Assistant Principal, limited competition entrant	3	2	2	4	8	5	5
Direct entrants to Principal grade	17	18	15	30	38	25	66
General and departmental Executive Class promotion	44	33	20	28	17	37	43*
Transfers and promotions from other Classes	8	4	5	4	9	13	1
Total	106	90	82	97	109	123	159

* Includes two who were first promoted to Assistant Principal.

The Civil Service Selection Board (c.s.s.b.) is the body responsible for arranging and conducting the selection process for entrants by open competition. The Board was modelled on the War Office Selection Board (w.o.s.b.) which during the Second World War evolved psychometric and other procedures to help them in selecting officers. Although there are still a number of similarities with w.o.s.b., c.s.s.b. has now become well established and widely known in its own right – at the present time over a thousand candidates for selection under a number of recruitment schemes pass through the Board each year. The organization at c.s.s.b. depends to a large extent on more than 70 part-time assessors, though there is a resident Directing Staff of five.

The c.s.s.b. procedure,[25] as far as the normal open competition to the Administrative Class is concerned, has a number of elements. First, there is pre-board information, which includes an outline of the candidate's career, referees' reports covering previous career and personality, marks in the qualifying examination and examiners' brief comments. Secondly, there is other information, arising mainly from individual discussions with interviewers (based both on topics the candidate has prepared and topics he has not prepared). Thirdly, there are the main tests which consist of practical exercises, psychometric tests (designed to measure intelligence, ability to think numerically, etc.) and interviews. c.s.s.b. collects all this information about each candidate and presents a report to the Final Selection Board.

The Civil Service Commission has made a number of follow-up studies on candidates recruited to the Service after having successfully passed through the selection procedures. The Commission reported in 1957 that between 1948 and 1956 Method I and Method II had attracted equal numbers of candidates for the Administrative Class, and the great majority of those successful by either method had proved entirely suitable. Because both methods of recruitment were attracting good candidates whose later careers indicated that they were capable of reaching the highest posts, it was decided that recruitment should be continued by both methods. However, after 1957 more and more candidates chose Method II. The Fulton Committee recommended that a special inquiry should be made of methods of selection, and this was done by a committee under the chairmanship of Mr J. G. W. Davies. As soon as the committee indicated that it had 'no doubts about the fairness of Method II', Lord Shackleton, who is in charge of the Civil Service Department, announced in May 1969 that that year's Method I examination would be the last.

The position of the civil servants who are transferred on promotion to the Administrative Class from other classes is one of special concern for the Treasury and Civil Service Commission because of the need to maintain similarly high standards in all Departments. The numbers involved in such promotions are far from insignificant as far as the class as a whole is concerned. When the Association of First Division Civil Servants recently conducted a survey[26] among a sample of its members it found that rather less than half had entered the Service as direct entrant Assistant Principals and a further 10 per cent as direct entry Principals. The remainder started their Civil Service careers in the Executive (10 per cent), Clerical (17 per cent) and Professional and Departmental Classes.

Treasury consent is necessary where promotions are made to the Administrative Class within Departments, and Departments are encouraged to invite the Civil Service Commission to be represented on their selection boards so that an even standard is maintained throughout the Service. The F.D.A. found in their survey that 23 per cent had joined the Class as a result of such departmental promotion.

In addition, a few entrants join as a result of inter-departmental promotion (arranged by the Civil Service Commission and Treasury in order to ensure opportunities to staff in Departments where there are no or very few Administrative posts) or transfers from other classes (such as by the special exercise held in 1964 which led to thirteen members of the Scientific Officer Class being appointed Principals).

The modes of entry to the Administrative Class for the civil servants surveyed by the F.D.A. were as follows:

TABLE VIII

MODE OF ENTRY TO ADMINISTRATIVE CLASS[27]

	Per cent
Open competition Method I	24
Open competition, Method II	26
Limited competition, Method I	2
Limited competition, Method II	8
Promotion within department	23
Late entry competition	8
Transfer from other class	3
Promotion between departments	2
Other	4
Total	100

Although such a significant proportion of the Administrative Class have been promoted or transferred from other classes, relatively few of them are likely to rise to the very highest positions – or, indeed, above the Administrative Class career grade of Assistant Secretary. This is shown in the following figures:

TABLE IX

GRADE OF JOINING CIVIL SERVICE[28]

(*in percentages*)

	Admin.	Exec.	Clerical	Stat.	Econ.	Dept. Exec.	Scientific	Works (inc. G.P.O.)	Other	Total
Grade now										
Principal	54	11	20	0	0	4	2	3	6	100
Assistant Secretary	55	10	16	0	1	8	1	2	7	100
Under Secretary	76	6	2	0	1	7	0	1	7	100
Total	56*	10	17	0	1	6	1	2	7	100

* 46 per cent of the total joined as A.P.s.

SUCCESSFULS AND UNSUCCESSFULS

The Civil Service Commission, in its concern for validity in selection procedures, has concentrated primarily on what has subsequently been thought of the prospects of a sample of those remaining in the Service. For example, evidence was prepared for the Fulton Committee, which showed the following statistics about entrants into the Administrative Class between 1948 and 1961 and who were still in the Service (316 were recruited by Method I and 229 by Method II).

	Present Performance		
	Very good indeed	Distinctly above average	Well-up-to-standard
Method I	4·1%	27·9%	54·7%
Method II	13·6%	39·3%	40·0%

13·3% of Method I candidates accordingly were thought to be below standard, and 6·1% of Method II candidates.

	Future Promise	
	A rank above Assistant Secretary	Assistant Secretary
Method I	31·0%	61·4%
Method II	48·9%	47·2%

Only 7·6% of Method I candidates and 3·9% of Method II candidates had therefore failed to fulfil the basic criterion of acceptability, a capacity of rising to Assistant Secretary.

The Civil Service Commission commented: 'In the most simplified of terms, these and other follow-up results indicate that the great majority of Method II entrants are regarded as satisfactory or better, that the number of "fliers" is encouraging, that relatively few are weak, but that the procedure has been insufficiently discriminating and that it has been over-severe in that a number of candidates who were not recommended would have done adequately had they been recommended.'[29]

This is one way of getting an impression of the validity of selection procedures. Such information suffers from the disadvantages of internal, subjective, staff assessments, though it may be useful for comparing the promise of different categories of entrant. A clearer indication may be provided by this information when it is considered alongside details that are known about the subsequent careers of those who were unsuccessful in the competition, together with attitudes towards the competition from both those who were successful and those who were unsuccessful. Fortunately, a certain amount of such information was also collected and presented in evidence to the Fulton Committee.

Dr J. F. Pickering, of the University of Sussex, made a survey[30] to investigate the careers of graduates who had thought of entering the Administrative Class of the Civil Service in 1951 (and had gone so far as to submit an application) but for one reason or another had not done so. Some withdrew before the competition, some were rejected as unsuitable, and others who were declared successful chose alternative careers. Another survey,[31] 'Profile of a Profession', by the present author, contributed to background information about Administrative Class civil servants through a cohort study of 1956 entrants.

Hardly any of the 1956 recruits had decided on their future career before attending university. Thirty-five completed the question on the questionnaire asking when they decided that they wanted to join the Civil Service, and the replies fell into the following categories:

(a) Before entry to university – 1.
('At no particular time . . . I had it in mind as a possible career before I went to Cambridge.')

(b) During undergraduate career, but before taking the Civil Service examinations – 17.
('At University – my tutor suggested that I ought to explore the Civil Service as a possible career.' 'While at University I decided I wanted to join the . . . [Ministry], but no other government department.' 'As a student . . . I wanted to "serve the community"; I wanted to avoid any scrambling for position etc. The Civil Service seemed the answer . . . [I also wanted to prove to myself that I could pass those Administrative examinations which are spoken of with bated breath].')

(c) During, or soon after the Civil Service examination – 6.
('During c.s.s.b. . . . I was impressed by the standard of the selection procedure.' 'In my last year at Cambridge *after* having sat the Civil Service examination and *after* having been offered a lectureship in classics.' 'I first took the Method II examination in a light-hearted way, having a first just behind me, with the intention of applying for the Foreign Office and at least partly with the idea of turning it down. They turned me down and I then had to consider the Home Civil Service for which I had been successful. My reasons for joining are coloured by hindsight, and drift played a large part.')

(d) While doing research – 5.
('While I was a research student I decided I did not want a University career.')

(e) After working for a time in industry – 2.
('Some time after graduating and after working in industrial management for about eighteen months.')

(f) After joining the Service – 2.
('About eighteen months after I had actually entered it . . . I joined because I had passed the examination.' 'Probably after I had done so. I was in some doubt when I entered and only did so because I was successful in getting into the . . . [Ministry], which attracted me for quite different reasons.')

(g) Other answers – 2.

('At no time did I take a positive decision.' 'I decided to apply by accident: it was a device for getting home a week or two earlier from West Africa [where I was doing national service].')

The hypothesis emerges that very few students go up to university with the intention of making a career in the higher Civil Service. This was confirmed by the survey carried out in 1967 for the Fulton Committee by the Psychological Research Centre. Their survey into student attitudes showed that 'apart from those choosing vocations such as teaching and social work, most students did not give serious consideration to a specific job until some time during their university course, mainly in their final year'.[32] It was therefore unreasonable to expect future candidates to select university courses with a view to their suitability for the subjects and syllabus of the Civil Service examinations. And any of these few who were primarily interested in sociology or social and public administration and chose to specialise in those subjects for their degrees would have found it almost impossible to select subjects in the Civil Service Method I open competition suitable for the studies they had pursued. Method II therefore became for them the only possible method of direct entry.

In addition, there appear to be a significant number of not unsuccessful administrative civil servants who drifted into the job, who did not make a positive decision for a career in the Civil Service, or who felt they made such a decision only *after* successfully completing the prestigious hurdle set by c.s.s.b.

It is also interesting to notice the alternative careers that 1956 entrants would have followed had they not joined the Civil Service. The overwhelming majority would have followed a university teaching career or entered some other form of public administration. A similar pattern is seen in the careers of the 'unsuccessfuls' where well over 50 per cent of those still employed are now teachers (in schools, further education and universities) or other forms of public administration. Furthermore, they appear to be very successful at it: for example, two-thirds of those who were teachers in institutions of further education in 1966 held senior positions and of the thirty university teachers in the sample, seven were professors, three were readers and five were senior lecturers.

THE PRESENT POSITION

Enthusiasts for the present Civil Service selection procedures argue that the method of open competition is sound, democratic and equitable in that it treats all comers alike, regardless of distinctions of wealth and social rank, in that it judges men and women impersonally by their ability to carry out a specific performance, and in that it selects individuals without reference to their family connections and inherited fortune, by the common rule of a prescribed test under known conditions. The procedures should, however, be carefully examined in the light of these criteria.

If the recruitment procedures are to be regarded as sound they must be tested for validity and reliability.

It is difficult to comment adequately on validity in the c.s.s.b. tests because the qualities sought by the Civil Service Commissioners are, to a large extent, confidential. Certain academic standards are assured by requiring all direct entrants to have at least a second-class honours degree and as the universities, through the appointment of external examiners and other means, do their best to ensure equality of standards, it must be assumed that all university degrees of a given standard are equivalent. Such a requirement is far from demanding, for examination results which place a student just within the category of lower second-class honours (a standard which should be well within the capacity of anyone admitted to a British university) thus give him the minimum academic requirement.

But any comment on whether the recruitment procedures measure what they are supposed to measure may be avoiding the question unless it is also concerned with whether the qualities sought are the ones most relevant for the work to be done. This is difficult because it brings into question the amount of research needed to investigate the most relevant qualities in applicants for management positions in both business and the public service. All that has so far been done to investigate this in Britain can be subsumed under memories and comments by serving and retired civil servants (some of whose writings and utterances may well be out of date by the time they are published), statements of what some people in the Civil Service think others in the Service are doing, an analysis made in 1945 of the work of Assistant Secretaries, and a couple of research studies for the Fulton Committee which at great speed tried to gather together some of the facts about what a sample of civil servants, almost minute in size and therefore statistically dubious, were actually doing at particular times. Given that insufficient is known about the work for which the selection procedures are designed, it seems rather futile to comment on whether the measurements of certain qualities do in fact reflect those abilities in the candidates being tested.

When c.s.s.b. was being evolved from w.s.o.b. it had the help of the conceptual thinking and practical experience of the psychologists who had developed many of the procedures in use for the armed forces. In addition, there were the results of the work carried out by Dr E. Anstey (with the help of Sir Cyril Burt) in 1945. He made a detailed analysis of the work performed by 505 Assistant Secretaries who had been asked to assess the relative importance of their various duties. From the analysis two factors emerged: (i) *concepts* (formulating policy, etc.) contrasted with *human affairs* (handling people and staff appraisal); (ii) work *inside* the Service (negotiations with representatives of other interests). Further processing of the data using these factors showed that the duties of Assistant Secretaries could be grouped into five main categories, but that well over half fell into the category 'general'. The results of this research are said to have helped significantly in decisions about the qualities to be sought in applicants for admission to the Administrative Class.[33]

Apart from the fact that not all members of the Administrative Class are Assistant Secretaries, that particular piece of research was carried out a quarter of a century ago and at a time when the Service was geared for war-time work (since 1945 c.s.s.b. has had to depend on other means for keeping in touch with the changes in Civil Service work). And G. K. Fry[34] has drawn attention to the important point that desirable qualities sought in an earlier period are not equally desirable or the most desirable qualities at the present time because the role of government is now much more positive. What we know higher civil servants actually do at the present time will be discussed in the next chapter, but it is significant how much of our knowledge still depends on what some civil servants *think* others are doing.

Doubts about this aspect of validity may also be responsible for a certain amount of 'playing safe' in selection procedures. The objective of the Administrative Class competition was explained in 1967 when the Civil Service Commission stated that 'the aim of the selection procedure is to test intellectual and personal qualities and to apply a uniform standard of assessment regardless of educational background'.[35] The Davies Committee in 1969 found that intellectual aptitude for the job remained the predominant requirement although 'personal and temperamental qualities are rightly given due weight in assessment'.[36] Several of the 1951 unsuccessfuls suggested that the selection procedure tended to favour candidates who were exclusively conformist. Another, who described himself as of the 'fellow traveller type', commented: 'The interviews that I had made it clear to me that my type was undesirable . . . This was one of the most horrible experiences of my life.'[37]

The difficulty of knowing what to look for, coupled with the characteristic c.s.s.b. type of thoroughness, is further emphasised by a comment from a 1966 candidate for the competition for Principals (age limits: 36–52 years). He said: 'The Civil Service would get more applications if they stopped asking for details of education, societies you belonged to at University, etc. The selection should be done by practical tests of administrative ability such as there have been in recent years. If the candidate is successful at these tests there is no need for anyone to know whether he acquired that ability at Tulse Hill or Tonbridge, whether he was a member of "Pop" or a "Half-blue".'[38]

As already mentioned, the Civil Service Commission, in making their own assessment of validity, relies to a large extent on performance and future promise in the Service. Though this may be interesting, it hardly solves the problem. For, given that entry into the Service at this level is strictly limited and there are only modest opportunities to move into or out of the Service later in a person's career, some must always be assumed as being in the top third and show promise for future promotion.

It is also difficult to make useful comments on the reliability of the recruitment procedures. This is partly because so few candidates make several attempts after once failing and in any case there is no means of finding out whether successful candidates in an expensive testing system would have done as well or better if tested more than once.

However, there is little doubt that the candidates themselves generally have a high opinion of the procedure and in particular have been very impressed by the c.s.s.b. tests and interviews.

It has already been mentioned that the high standard set by c.s.s.b.

E

was an important factor in the decision to enter the Service for at least one of the 1956 entrants. In fact, twenty-four of the thirty-two 1956 entrants interviewed[39] said they were attracted to the entry competition by the fact that it was difficult to pass and they took the examination simply for the fun of it, so that they could compete against their contemporaries, but then, when they had been offered a place by the Civil Service Commission, they felt they could not turn it down simply because they had passed the examination against stiff competition. Twenty-four of the thirty-two said they had *not* been attracted by the idea that if they passed the examinations and were offered a place they would be joining some kind of élite. Of the eight others, one said that this had been an element 'but it was an élite of yesterday rather than today', and three more added that although this element had attracted them, they had since been rather disappointed about this aspect of the Civil Service and did not now feel part of an élite.

Despite the comments of the 1956 entrants, it is interesting to notice that the competition has, in some respects, the aura of an initiation ceremony. It may also be classed as a variety of what Eric Berne has called the game of 'Look Ma no Hands'.[40]

Favourable comments about c.s.s.b. have also been made by those who competed but were unsuccessful and this is particularly impressive when coming from members of a group who might be expected to harbour 'sour grapes'. Of the 1951 unsuccessfuls surveyed by J. F. Pickering, several remarked that they were pleased not to have been selected as they now felt that they were not best suited for a career in the Civil Service.

An interesting sidelight is shed on the type of person attracted to the Administrative Class by considering possible alternative careers considered by the 1956 entrants. The 1956 group were asked: 'If you had not entered the Civil Service, what career would you have followed?' The answers were classified as:

University teaching	17
Industry or management	7
Other public administration	5
Law	4
Miscellaneous	3
Don't know	2

It is sometimes suggested that top civil servants are like successful business managers and therefore they should receive similar pay, but it seems that very few serving civil servants represent losses to industry. As A. H. Halsey and I. M. Crewe have observed, what in fact stands out when a pay-comparison is made with academics is the existence of 15% of the Administrative Class posts (Under Secretary and above) beyond the range of a university professorship; and 47% beyond that of a senior lectureship. Moreover, the salary of a Principal in the Civil Service for a man aged thirty or less compares very favourably with normal alternative opportunities in the universities and industry. Against this has to be set the wider opportunities for supplementary earnings which are open to dons and closed to civil servants (but academic supplementary earnings are significant for only a small minority).[41]

If they had not been appointed to the Civil Service the chances appear high that many Administrative Class civil servants would have entered some other form of public service. There may well be a psychological type of person attracted to Civil Service work – though research may demonstrate that such a type has few characteristics in common with the caricatured civil servant of novels, music-hall jokes and cartoons. One civil servant may recently have given an introduction to this possible psychological type when he explained his reason for choosing the Civil Service as a career. He wrote: 'I did not feel it as a vocation before I entered. . . . I had no wish to enter advertising or industry, since I lack the qualities of brashness and bonhomie which seem to be needed. Other professions I had not considered. I am too squeamish and unscientific to become a doctor or dentist, too unsympathetic to figures to make them my livelihood as an accountant, even if I use them in much of my work.'[42]

An examination of the educational backgrounds of those recently recruited may also suggest characteristics of the sort of person attracted to the Service. Of the 1956 entrants, seventeen out of thirty-five read history at university and the next most popular subjects were economics and classics with only three each. The Civil Service Commission produced figures for the Fulton Committee showing applications for the Administrative Class compared with university output of graduates in groups of subjects and found that the Administrative Class is most attractive to Arts graduates from Oxford and Cambridge, particularly those reading history and classics.[43] It is not, therefore, surprising that Arts graduates form the majority of the total intake. In 1965, 75 per cent of the successful candidates had read Arts (85 per cent in 1964 and 76 per cent up to September 1966), and Arts graduates also constituted 68 per cent of all successful candidates during the period 1948–63. Furthermore, the proportion of these candidates who had read history was consistently large (in 1964, 40 per cent; in 1965, 45 per cent; and in 1966, 37 per cent).

The 1956 entrants also usefully commented on their educational background before joining the Service. Of thirty-five entrants in that year, fourteen took their first degrees at Cambridge, nine at Oxford, four at London, two each at Edinburgh and St Andrews, and one each at Aberdeen, Glasgow, Liverpool and Manchester. The class of honours and main subject studied in their first degrees were as follows:

Class of degree honours		Subject of degree	
1st	20	History	17
2nd	14	Economics	3
3rd	1	Classics	3
		English	2
		Jurisprudence	2
		Modern Languages	2
		P.P.E. (Oxford)	2
		Government (B.Sc. Econ. London)	2
		Philosophy+Politics	1
		Modern History+Political Economy	1

Nine out of the thirty-five had been awarded further degrees or diplomas by 1966 or had done more than a year's full-time research at a university. These included two Ph.D.s, and one each B.Phil., M.Litt., B.C.L. and a Diploma in Public and Social Administration. Nearly all felt their education prior to joining the Civil Service had been a very good background for their work. However, twelve out of thirty-two answering the question added that they would have found a study of economics and public and political institutions very useful indeed (these were apart from the five with degrees in economics or P.P.E.).

The predominance of successful candidates from Oxford and Cambridge over candidates from all other universities is still a matter for criticism because, even when it does not lead to allegations of intentional bias through the selection procedure, it stimulates questions about recruitment policy (it emphasises, for example, the importance of deciding to which university to apply at a time when most young people have little idea about their post-university careers). In the early 1960s, when it might have been thought that there would be more successes from non-Oxbridge universities, the figures show the contrary. In the period 1957–63, 85 per cent of open competition direct entrants had Oxbridge degrees, but in 1948–56 the proportion was only 78 per cent (and in H. E. Dale's sample of the higher Civil Service shortly before the Second World War, the proportion was 68 per cent). Far from improving, the figures were therefore worsening: as the number of graduates went up each year, and as the proportion from other universities increased, there was a general tendency for the proportion of Administrative Class successes from Oxbridge also to go up. However, the figures have more recently shown a tendency in the other direction and the general picture of recruitment by Method II has been of a movement away from the overwhelming preponderance of Oxford and Cambridge and traditional arts degrees, though these categories still produce the majority of successful candidates.[44] In 1968, 59 per cent of all direct entrants (Method I and Method II together) to the Administrative Class had degrees from Oxford or Cambridge universities[45] (but this figure is a long way from matching the drop in the proportion of students graduating from Oxford and Cambridge: in 1938–39 it was 22 per cent, but in 1963–64 it was 14 per cent).[46]

Criticisms of the selection procedure only scratch the surface of the problem. It is not surprising, however, that this criticism exists, for it is factually based, whereas an overall picture of what Administrative civil servants actually do still depends to a remarkable extent on conjecture.

4. The Work They Do

'To the general public, indeed, the adoption of open competition in 1870 seemed to obviate any necessity for further consideration not only of the method by which officials were appointed but also of the system under which they did their work. . . . Appointment was to be by "merit", and the announcement of the examination results, like the wedding in a middle-Victorian novel, was to be the end of the story.'[1]

TYPE OF WORK

'You will spend a fair amount of time in your office writing and answering letters to members of the public, other civil servants, outside bodies with which your department deals; preparing memoranda, writing minutes, suggesting how to initiate, implement or alter policy; telephoning or being telephoned: interviewing visitors; discussing informally with colleagues how or what to do; consulting the specialists with whom the Administrative civil servant has more and more contact: architects, surveyors, engineers, cost accountants, doctors, inspectors of several kinds. In many departments of government Principals and some Assistant Secretaries have territorial responsibilities which necessitate periodic visits away from the office. These visits can refresh as well as inform. In this age of government by committee, you will have to attend at committees in your own department as secretary or member or assessor or chairman, at inter-departmental committees or at an outside body's committee as your department's representative. An ability to speak intelligibly, briefly and cogently is needed in the Home Civil Service just as much as in the Foreign Service. The opportunities for foreign travel tend to grow, even in social service departments; for we are all internationally minded now. In my own short period of service I have attended two international conferences, and I see an appreciable number of foreign visitors who tend to include a visit to a Ministry if they are studying any aspect of administration.'[2]

That was how William Reid, then a recently promoted Principal, described in a careers symposium, the sort of work he did as an Administrative civil servant. It is quoted here partly because it is a well-written account from his own experience and is typical of the variety of work carried out in the Administrative Class at the present time, but primarily because there is no better description available of ordinary Administrative Class work. This account may be linked on the one hand with what has already been said – especially in chapter 2 on the I.C.S. – about the variety of work that may be encountered. It may also be linked to the selection procedure as discussed in chapter 3.

C. H. Sisson has drawn attention to the significance of certain instructions produced by the Civil Service Commission about their own selection procedures: 'In their notes on both Method I and Method II the Civil Service Commission have a sentence, the repetition of which suggests what general importance they attach to it, which reads: "Work in all subjects should be expressed clearly and concisely in good English". It is as if it did not matter what one knew as long as one could explain clearly what it was. . . . The candidate has to be able to have "grasp of the material", "to think constructively, to reason". But as to what he is to reason about, let him, as the candidates under Method II are specifically invited to do, "choose freely what aspects of the subject" already elected by them "they will develop and how widely they will range in it". . . . The philosophy of the competition finds perfect expression in the words used to describe the Intelligence Test under Method II. "This", says the explanatory note sublimely, "is a test of mental ability." '[3]

The hypothesis therefore emerges that Administrative civil servants, who number about three thousand people, are grouped into one class for which the method of selection is one of the most significant experiences the majority have in common, and do work which is almost infinitely various. Furthermore, the selection procedure itself, rigorous but general, may be the supreme example of 'playing safe'. Fortunately, however, more is now generally known about work in the higher Civil Service than was known, say, five years ago.

The Fulton Committee instituted two surveys which included investigations into what Administrative Class civil servants actually do. One was a survey based on 1956 direct entrants into the Administrative Class[4] and the other was the Management Consultancy

Group's investigation of blocks of Civil Service work. In addition, the Association of First Division Civil Servants instituted their own survey among members.

Two ways of classifying their work were suggested to the 1956 sample. One appeared on the questionnaire as: 'Would you describe the work you do as a civil servant as primarily (a) executive management, (b) policy formation, (c) regulatory work, (d) negotiation, (e) other?' The answers were as follows:

Executive management	5
Policy formation	15
Regulatory work	1
Negotiation	3
Other	8

Note: Where two categories were chosen in answer to this question and marked as of equal importance a half-point has been allotted to each in the above table.

However, it must be stressed that those answers tended to be given only with a great deal of qualification which suggests the form of classification is very imperfect. Two examples will illustrate this: 'It depends on the field of work. In my last post (b), (c) and (d) were predominant – but in my present post (a) and (d). This reflects the very wide division in the work of the Service between the traditional policy formation and regulatory work (often closely associated with Ministers and Parliament) and the growing field of executive management of practical tasks (often of great magnitude).' 'The work *I* do at the moment is very un-typical Principal work. It is a mixture of (b) and (d). I have no money or powers to do anything; I work through organizations (some independent, some government financed) and have to try to do policy-planning by discussion, manipulation and purse-string coercion etc.' Several of the civil servants who said their work was *primarily* (b), (c), (d) or (e) above, pointed out that management is a significant part of the work of the Administrative Class, but that as such it was not appreciated.

The second way of classifying work done was based on categories mentioned by H. E. Dale. The question appeared on the questionnaire as: 'The following is a list of the types of work you may be doing. Please write 1, 2, 3 etc. against them in the order in which they make demands on your time (so that No. 1 will be the most time-consuming for you, No. 2 the next time-consuming and so on):

'(i) Giving written instructions concerning matters submitted to you by your subordinates and which are to be passed no higher.

'(ii) Writing your own minutes, memoranda or letters to indicate your views on matters submitted by your subordinates and which are to be passed to higher authority.

'(iii) Writing minutes, memoranda or letters on matters referred to you by your official superiors (whether or not you pass them to subordinates).

'(iv) Interviews and telephone conversations with people both inside and outside the Civil Service.

'(v) Miscellaneous work not falling under the headings enumerated above.'

This appeared a straightforward and easy way of classifying work but, though it was an abbreviation of what Dale said civil servants did in their daily life in the office, it was virtually irrelevant thirty years later, in 1966. The replies were so qualified and annotated that they were completely unclassifiable.

The reason for the irrelevance of Dale's classification is interesting. According to the civil servants the grouping is deceptively simple and makes no allowance for the much greater involvement of contemporary government with almost every organization in the country. For example, Dale's classification does not bring out the extent to which so many Administrative civil servants now deal directly with outside organizations. This results in work that has neither come up nor down in the hierarchy, yet can often be so time-consuming that it would have to be classed first of the five categories. Another development since Dale wrote is in special sorts of work generated by government policies of devolution to the regions – this may result in, for example, work with financial controls exercised by government on the regions. Some of the 1956 sample also made the point that a lot of their time was spent on background reading, or involved studying and analysing problems. Others made the point that in their jobs they were in fact *originating* work.

The survey also found that the nature of the work of Principals is such that most people find its intrinsic quality makes only a moderate demand on their ability. However, twelve out of the thirty-two said their present work made a great demand on their ability and ten of the twelve added that this was primarily because of the time factor: 'The work is a great demand on physical stamina and quick-wittedness'; 'One has to be able to work long and hard under pressure'. Four of the thirty-two said that their work was making only a slight demand on their ability, and a few more said they had *recently* been doing work which had been very undemanding.

The civil servants were also questioned about the demands of their work in terms of time. Most of them are usually in the office from about 9.45 a.m. to 7 p.m., and in addition take home about five hours work each week, but an average working week of about 55 hours in the office is not unusual.

However, all recognised that their work was such that they had to work hours appropriate to its demands, and it is not unusual for them to be very hard pressed from time to time. For example, one civil servant recalled that during the economic crisis in 1964 he worked regularly from 9.00 a.m. to 7.00 p.m. and took home about twenty hours of work each week. Another, concerned with the Rhodesian crisis at the time he was interviewed, gave details of the hours he had worked in Downing Street during that week and they amounted to about seventy-five hours. Private Secretaries, of whom there were three in the sample, may expect to work a regular sixty-hour week.

The Management Consultancy Group was appointed by the Fulton Committee to examine a number of blocks of Civil Service work to find out what civil servants were actually doing, what amounts and kinds of responsibility they held and skills the work called for, and how civil servants of various classes worked together. The Group saw 77 members of the Administrative Class from the grades of Assistant Principal to Under Secretary.

They found that administrative civil servants were:

'(a) forecasting expenditure;
(b) exercising financial and other control over the work of Departments, including the work of government architects, engineers and other specialists;
(c) reviewing the investment programmes of the nationalised industries;
(d) recommending, or advising on, new policies and policy options and writing appropriate papers;

(e) preparing legislation in consultation with members of the legal class;

(f) negotiating with local authorities, nationalised industries, private industry and members of the public on matters concerning the operation of existing government policies and on new policies and regulations;

(g) preparing explanatory briefs on current policy;

(h) preparing material for ministerial speeches;

(i) preparing answers to Parliamentary Questions and to letters from M.P.s etc.;

(j) making decisions on individual casework arising from legislation;

(k) acting as chairmen and secretaries of, and representatives on, Departmental and Inter-Departmental Committees;

(l) directing and operating Establishments Divisions;

(m) managing large blocks of staff.'[5]

Three specific examples of Administrative Class work studied by the Management Consultancy Group illustrate how this works out in practice:

'. . . Each year the policy branches of the Department of Education and Science provide Finance Branch with forecasts of future numbers of pupils, teachers and so on, together with estimates of the additional places in schools and other educational institutions required to provide for rising numbers. Finance Branch checks these forecasts for internal consistency, where necessary takes up doubtful points with the branches concerned and converts the figures into year-by-year estimates of expenditure, both current and capital, over five years. These estimates are then discussed in detail with the Treasury, with the object of producing an agreed report for Ministers on the cost of the continuation of current policies. This report, with those prepared for other services, forms the basis of annual Cabinet decisions on expenditure. During the ministerial discussions the Branch has to brief the Secretary of State, and if necessary draft papers for circulation to the Cabinet or a Cabinet Committee, on the details of educational expenditure, particularly the more controversial items. Similarly the Branch provides him with an analysis of the expenditure forecasts for other services so that he can compare rates of growth and, together with the economists in the Department's Planning Branch, prepare critical commentaries on the estimates of economic growth etc.

prepared by the Treasury and the Department of Economic Affairs. All this work occupies the time of several members of the Branch for a substantial part of the year. Once expenditure limits have been settled by Ministers, the Branch is responsible for applying them both to the Department's Estimates for the immediately following year and to the two-year forecasts of expenditure submitted by local authorities for the purposes of rate support grant. The second of these operations, a two-yearly one, requires the Branch to make detailed comparisons of the forecasts both of numbers of pupils and teachers etc. submitted by the local authorities and of their forecasts of expenditure, and also involves an assessment of the rate at which, in relation to Ministers' decisions, costs per pupil or student can be allowed to rise. Detailed papers are circulated to the local authority associations as a preliminary to discussion with them: the final stages are meetings between the associations and the Ministers responsible for local authority services and the briefing of Ministers for a debate on the Rate Support Grant Order laid before Parliament by the Minister of Housing.

'Within the framework of Parliamentary and Treasury control responsibility for department expenditure rests with the Permanent Secretary in his role as Departmental Accounting Officer. This responsibility is exercised on his behalf at appropriate levels within the Administrative and Executive chain where proposals for individual items of expenditure are critically examined. In the areas of work which we saw the control over expenditure was being exercised by Administrative and Executive staff employed in administrative divisions headed by Assistant Secretaries. For example, in the Ministry of Public Buildings and Works, estimates of cost and detailed designs prepared by the specialist staff for all naval installations, including submarine pens, medical facilities and housing, had to be submitted to the appropriate administrative divisions for vetting and financial approval. In the Ministry of Transport the same procedures applied to submissions for expenditure on motorways, including service areas and flyover junctions.'[6]

'Legislation often creates a great deal of individual casework. Distribution of Industry legislation is a good example of this. Broadly, Board of Trade policy is to steer industrial development to areas of high unemployment and to restrain such development in areas of labour shortage in the Midlands and South East. This involves the

Department in detailed consultations with a very large number of firms. The smaller and more straightforward cases are dealt with in the Board's regional offices. The more important and complicated cases are referred to headquarters. We saw one Assistant Secretary in the Distribution of Industry Division who spent some two-thirds of his time dealing with individual firms, trying to deflect them from expanding their operations in areas of full employment and encouraging them to go to the less prosperous areas instead. A Principal was also spending about half his time on this activity. In the same Division, applications for building grants were dealt with by executive staff who referred to the Administrators all individual applications not covered by established precedents. One issue arising out of this and being dealt with by Administrators involved a decision on whether, within existing legislation, such establishments as night clubs should be eligible for building grants. This was not a trivial matter. The point to be decided was to what extent the Department should be involved in financing the improvement of the social infrastructure of Development Districts. Administrators also become involved in cases where there is political sensitivity or where representations have been made at a high level.'[7]

'A feature of all the Departments we saw was a central Establishment Division, headed by a Principal Establishment Officer who was a member of the Administrative Class, usually at the Under Secretary level. Examples of the tasks being undertaken by Administrators in Establishment Divisions were chairing promotion boards, dealing with disciplinary cases and arranging individual postings. One Under Secretary chaired all promotion boards dealing with promotions from Senior Executive Officer to Chief Executive Officer and usually sat on Civil Service Commission Boards for all appointments of professional staff in his Department. He saw all promotion board reports, some 180 a year, and examined the annual reports of some 800 staff. He was also concerned with difficult discipline cases – for example, he was considering the case of a middle-aged but comparatively junior officer who was about to be retired prematurely because of the trouble he created with his colleagues. In addition, at the Under Secretary level considerable time is given to the consideration of the careers of individual members of the Administrative Class. Other work of Administrators in Establishment Divisions includes forecasting staff requirements, considering requests for additional staff and negotiating with staff associations. Principal Establishments Officers are also usually responsible for departmental efficiency in that they direct departmental staff inspection and organization and methods sections.

'Two of the Under Secretaries we saw were in charge of very large blocks of staff. The Controller, Ministry of Social Security, Newcastle, managed an establishment of some 9,500 staff, mostly engaged on clerical work but including very large computer installations. The Under Secretary in charge of the Contracts Division of the Ministry of Technology headed a block of about 1,550 staff including executives, accountants, engineers and technical grades. These two jobs, both from the point of view of numbers of staff involved and the management techniques employed, appeared to us to be comparable with top management in industry. Excluding Establishment posts, the other Under Secretaries we saw were in charge of smaller groups of staff, ranging from 18 to 360. At Assistant Secretary level the groups under command ranged from 4 to 89; at the Principal level they averaged 6.'[8]

In their survey, the Association of First Division Civil Servants asked respondents to indicate the proportions of their time spent on each of nine different types of activities. The break-down into categories was rather different from that presented to the 1956 entrants, but the question was essentially similar. Perhaps the most interesting result was that 'a number of people had found it difficult to break down their work in the way requested',[9] thus confirming the general conclusion presented in 'Profile of a Profession'.

What emerges from such recent investigations into what Administrative civil servants do is a very patchy picture. The Treasury manual on establishments work, 'Estacode', accepts the formulation of the Reorganization Committee of 1920–21 and defines the general duties of the Administrative Class as the formulation of policy, the co-ordination and improvement of government machinery and the general administration and control of the departments of the public service.[10] As a general description this may be adequate, but it cannot be denied that it is also vague.

The 'Estacode' description has, however, to be vague at the present time because on the one hand Administrative Class work involves many quite different types of work and on the other no really comprehensive survey and analysis has been made to classify what is being done by these people. There were only about thirty-five civil servants in the 1966 survey for 'Profile of a Profession' and seventy-seven administrators in the survey of the Management Consultancy Group's investigation. A more comprehensive research study of what Administrative civil servants do in the Service as a whole is clearly needed. Departmental establishments officers may have a reasonably accurate idea of what is done in their particular departments, but there is considerable variation from department to department and the image inside each particular department may be considerably influenced by 'the departmental view'.

This is well illustrated by the replies of the 1956 entrants when they were asked to state, with reasons, which three departments in their opinions were the most attractive and which three were the least attractive to work in. A very large majority stated that they felt these were impossible questions to answer because all departments have both attractive and unattractive jobs in them, and the departmental subject matter of Civil Service work is relatively unimportant in making particular posts or departments attractive. Although answers given were almost unclassifiable because so many significant comments qualified the choices given, they were interesting for three reasons. First, nearly everyone in the sample included his own department as being attractive – mainly because the work and people were familiar but also because civil servants tend to feel very ignorant of what goes on in other departments. Secondly, two departments emerged, even through the claims of ignorance, with a very attractive image, the Treasury and the Department of Economic Affairs, and two emerged as very unattractive – the Ministries of Social Security and Defence. Thirdly, the main qualities that make a department appear attractive are: (a) the importance of the work involved; (b) interesting subject matter and variety of subject matter; (c) people already in the department give the impression of being intellectually stimulating people to work with. The main qualities that make a department unattractive are: (a) work that seems to be mainly executive in character, and/or (b) work that seems to be more concerned with destruction than construction.

There is, therefore, in the Service as a whole, still a great deal of reliance on personal impressions of what some civil servants think others are doing, and these are unreliable because the experience on which the generalisations are based is not sufficiently wide nor is it sufficiently recent. This lack of information (remembering that, apart from the 1945 analysis of the work of Assistant Secretaries mentioned in the previous chapter, there were no similar surveys before those commissioned by the Fulton Committee) also casts serious doubts on the present grading structure at higher levels in the Service.

TRAINING

There are considerable variations in the extent and quality of training in different departments. There are also considerable variations between the present training situation as explained by the Treasury to the Fulton Committee and the experience of those members of the Administrative Class involved in surveys and investigations for the Fulton Committee. The main reason for this appears to be that training programmes referred to by the Treasury have been only recently introduced so civil servants who have benefited have tended to be the more recent recruits, whereas those surveyed for 'Profile of a Profession' had been in the Service for ten years and unfortunately missed most of the training programmes, and those surveyed by the Management Consultancy Group included civil servants at all stages in their careers.

As far as the Civil Service is concerned, training can be considered in two categories. First, there is the traditional training experienced by British civil servants which should more appropriately be regarded as a process of socialisation. Secondly, there are the formal training programmes associated with the growing awareness of the need for management training for civil servants which could be recognised in the late 1950s, and received impetus from the publication of the Plowden Report on Control of Expenditure in 1961 which drew attention to the extent to which many civil servants are involved in management.

Consider, first, the post-entry socialisation process.

This was to a large extent a process of non-training because there was very little in the way of a planned training schedule, or, indeed, much attention paid to any aspect of management in the more technical sense of the word. It depended on regular postings so that the new recruit, if fortunate, would spend, perhaps, five or six years being posted at regular intervals to various branches within a Ministry. It is sometimes called on-the-job training or 'sitting with Nellie', and its advocates have believed that the only way to learn how to do Civil Service work is by doing it. It is almost certain that it has its origins in the extraordinary variety of work encountered by members of the Indian Civil Service in the last century, but also to a lesser extent in the continuing variety of work associated with the Administrative Class of the Home Civil Service in more recent times. The problem has been how to introduce the new recruit successfully to the acceptable way of dealing with problems of the public service. The solution in India was one that resembled trial by water: the new entrant was pushed into a particular situation and if he survived he and the service were both better off; if he didn't survive he was replaced by someone else sent out from the old country. The solution in the Home Civil Service was that the new entrant should be launched more gently by giving him a period of induction during which he watched serving officers carry out their duties, then letting him work on his own.

At the beginning of this century the procedure was clearly explained to the MacDonnell Royal Commission on the Civil Service. Sir Robert Chalmers, then Permanent Secretary to the Treasury, was asked by Philip Snowden: 'When a young fellow comes fresh from success in the Class I examination say, to the Treasury, what is the kind of work to which you first put him?' He replied:

'I will tell the honourable member, with reference to the cases of two men who got in in the last examination . . . I am very interested indeed in seeing that they do get what I regard as the best training we can give. I put one where he would have a great amount of work that would regularise his mind in the way of accuracy; that is the chief thing to begin with with every officer entering my department; and he has to deal with superannuations, which involve a great mass of statutes and a great mass of precedents, and with the certainty that mistakes will be detected later in quite a large proportion, if they occur, by the Audit Office. In my mind it is a peculiarly useful thing to get a man accurate and at the same time capable of dealing with the subject as a whole, in order to get a good general basis of training. The other one I put in another division, the financial division, and he has to do things which are somewhat comparable to the super-annuation papers. He would deal with a certain amount of drudgery, which is deliberately put upon a junior in that division; all the travelling claims, for instance, of honourable members of this Commission

F

he has to check and see that they are right; and if they are wrong, and that is detected by the Audit Office, he has to put them right. That is a very salutary training for a young man. That is one small branch of his work in order to test accuracy. On the other hand, he has to do work on currency matters, either currency or banking, or things related to Estimates. There are two or three juniors, and I forget which particular branch this man does; but he will go through all of them. At the end of a couple of years in both those divisions I regard a junior as having become a trained official; then he tends to move from one place to another every year.'[11]

Although this description was given at the beginning of the century it has proved not untypical of twentieth-century training. Indeed, the training received in the Treasury during Chalmers' time might have been envied by others less fortunate in other departments. C. K. Munro, for example, has explained that when he joined the Board of Trade he was taken to a room bare of everything except a table, a chair, and a telephone, given a fat file of papers and told to see what he could make of it: that was the only formal instruction he received.[12]

When the 1956 entrants were surveyed for the Fulton Committee, it was found that during their ten years in the Service all had obtained a fairly wide range of experience within their departments and had been given new postings at an average of about one a year (though some people in the larger departments tended to have postings every six months during their period as Assistant Principals). Generally speaking, after promotion to Principal, their postings averaged out at about a new posting every eighteen months to two years. Those serving in large departments said the planned regular postings during their period as an A.P., sometimes with a regional tour as well, were very profitable, assuming they remained with that department. A couple of the civil servants recalled that 'the best of my training was serving in a Minister's Private Office for a year and a half' and others commented that 'training on the job can be very valuable if you have a good teacher . . . but not everyone is a good teacher'.

The Management Consultancy Group found that some civil servants complained of having nothing to do during their induction or training period; they also tended to be supernumerary, having no specific job but being dependent for the quality and quantity of their day-to-day work on the interest shown by their immediate supervisors and the readiness of the supervisors to delegate. It is not surprising that such experience tends to cause frustration among recent entrants (though there was compensation for their frustration in the bright career prospect – virtually all Assistant Principals can expect to become Principals at 27–28 years of age, on a salary scale of £2,724– £3,721, and Assistant Secretaries at about 40 on a salary scale of £4,170–£5,325).

On-the-job training may, in practice, be less important for learning the work than it is for socialisation – that is, learning attitudes of mind, accepted codes of behaviour, knowing what is done and what is not done; where each civil servant has the opportunity to form in his own mind a fairly indelible mental picture of the ideal civil servant.

This socialisation process appears to contribute to and help perpetuate the popular image of the Civil Service. It produces a mental picture of how civil servants should appear, as well as how they should act, which may have a quite remarkable effect on some civil servants. One may notice, for example, that a large proportion of senior civil servants choose to wear the same somewhat neutral style of Oxford shoes (usually black – a plain shoe with a toe-cap). There is a sort of atmosphere in the corridors of a major department of state, which is noticeable in modes of behaviour and attitudes of mind as well as in the traditional colours of paintwork and the characteristic hint of detergent or floor polish.

Yet the significance of the socialisation process may also be more fundamental. It may instil acceptable codes of behaviour which can be applied to the use of bureaucratic power in individual circumstances. It may temper or re-direct possible excesses of bureaucratic power. It may have an effect similar to the secluded upbringing of Plato's guardians, and it would certainly be valuable to study in depth just how important this process is in formulating in senior administrators attitudes of mind consistent with the British system of government. When one knows individually a number of higher civil servants one tends to regard them as individual persons, and it is then less easy to regard them collectively as a group with certain characteristics and interests in common. Yet one has the impression that these characteristics do exist and that they include an unemotional concern in relation to individuals and circumstances, a peculiar tact and sometimes an inscrutable caution. These characteristics can, perhaps, be most easily appreciated when seen in the context of the system of government, for some of the qualities are consistent with Max Weber's ideal type of bureaucracy (where, for example, the individual conducts his office in a spirit of formalistic impersonality) and others with certain of the conventions of the British constitution (for example, the conventional doctrine of ministerial responsibility).

The importance of this matter cannot be over-simplified. Whilst there is no serious problem of corruption in the British Civil Service, the problem of the balance of power in our system of government may be even more dangerous and insidious. And one aspect of this problem is that not enough is known about these traditional, so-called training, procedures.

When Mr A. S. Melford Stevenson was conducting the case for Lieutenant Commander Marten in the Crichel Down affair, he looked for the thread which linked the very different officials involved. They had no corrupt motive, but all of them were prepared to do and say things which, he said, persons of their position and background would never do in the normal course of behaviour. Manifestly, Mr Stevenson concluded, they derived great satisfaction from the exercise of personal power which they were able to wield at the expense of somebody else's pocket. 'There is a time,' he declared, 'when the public administrator can become, if not drunk, unfit to be in charge of his personal power. You may think that the conduct in this case exhibited by so many people suggests that that may be the common link which binds them and which explains the odd story that has been revealed.'[13]

This illustrates how important it may be to know the significance of the socialisation process as it has for long operated in the British Civil Service, and as it continues to operate, with certain modifications, at present. The important and interesting training programmes instituted in recent years may then be tailored to fit in with other aspects of the induction process.

Despite its history, according to the Management Consultancy Group, the Civil Service now provides for its staff more training than is general in industry – the Group came across a number of excellent training schemes during their investigation, and also concluded that the course now given to Assistant Principals at the Centre for Administrative Studies 'seemed . . . to compare favourably with the formal training that is generally given to their counterparts in industry.'[14]

Formal training for Administrative civil servants in Britain is provided in one of four ways:[15] (i) Departmentally, either by some form of training on the job including programmed instruction, or by a Departmental course; (ii) a central course sponsored by the Civil Service Department (this includes the Centre for Administrative Studies, the Civil Service College at Sunningdale and the c.s.c. centre in Edinburgh); (iii) by sending civil servants on external courses arranged for and attended by students from other occupations (such as the Administrative Staff College at Henley, the Institute of Local Government Studies in Birmingham University and the Business Schools); (iv) by commissioning outside organizations to plan and run courses specially for civil servants. It must, however, be stressed that all these types of formal training are fairly new.

Civil Service training within departments is not so new as the other forms, if the socialisation already referred to is considered as training. In some departments it is, however, coupled with a degree of planned posting or other induction training which together can be highly regarded by the Administrative Class civil servants who experience it. For example, one of the 1956 entrants serving in the Post Office, who spent her period as an Assistant Principal being posted at almost six-monthly intervals, was given the opportunity to do work at various levels in the organization (including work in the lower grades of the Executive Class) and said that she subsequently found it most helpful – but the Post Office tended to be more concerned about training than most other departments, particularly the smaller ones.

Where such planned posting includes a period in the Private Office this also is greatly appreciated by those experiencing it as it affords a valuable opportunity to get a bird's-eye view of all aspects of the department's work. As far as departmental training courses are concerned, these are rarely provided for Administrative civil servants partly because the overall numbers in most departments are too few to make it worthwhile, but partly also because there is too great a variety of work for Administrative civil servants at any level of the hierarchy to make it possible to arrange a course in sufficient depth in any particular specialist field.

Centralised courses for Administrative civil servants have improved enormously in recent years. Many in the middle and upper grades of the Class have still, however, missed out on such courses, yet it is they who are and will be taking the burden of the heaviest responsibilities in the higher Civil Service at present and in the immediate future.

The experiences of the 1956 entrants has been quite typical; they had almost no formal training for the work they were doing in the mid 1960s. Twenty-six out of thirty-two remembered spending three weeks very early in their careers on a low level Treasury course which one of them described as 'a child's guide to government and administration' – the other six did not even attend that course (they included one who explained 'I was put on the three-week A.P. course run by the Treasury but taken off after a day because of urgent departmental work'). The usual story was one of 'I spent a day being shown round the department on arrival and three weeks later I was on the three-week A.P. course'. Three of the thirty-two had at some stage attended a two-week course at the Centre for Administrative Studies (one more was proposed for the C.A.S. course but had to withdraw because of work pressure), two had spent a sabbatical year in the U.S.A. (on Harkness Fellowships) and one had spent three months at the Henley Administrative Staff College. Five of the 1956 entrants, who began their careers in very large departments, attended departmental introduction courses lasting about a week. But that was the total training during a period of ten years in the Service for the thirty-two civil servants concerned.

Nearly everyone condemned the Treasury course they attended in such terms as 'of no value whatever', 'a complete waste of time' or 'as satisfactory as a three-week introductory course could be'. The only point mentioned in its favour was that it enabled fairly isolated civil servants to meet other new entrants of similar age from other departments. The Treasury courses as experienced by the 1956 entrants have since been replaced by the expanded course for Assistant Principals at the Centre for Administrative Studies. One civil servant, expressing the sentiments of many in the group, said 'I would have welcomed the opportunity to attend the present A.P.s' course at the C.A.S. . . . many of us need to know about modern techniques of management and administration.'

In more recent years the position for new entrants has, however, considerably improved. Following recommendations in two reports prepared in 1962[16] the Centre for Administrative Studies was established in 1963 in two houses in Regent's Park, London, and admitted its first course in October of that year. The directing staff now consists of an Assistant Secretary, a full-time economist, and two Principals. Most of the teaching is by university teachers from a number of universities, plus some sessions from civil servants and management consultants.

Its main course has developed into one which now lasts 28 weeks and, since 1966, has been held three times a year. A survey of the content of this course is given in Table X, on the next page, and the Fulton Committee was told that:

'The structure of the course has developed to secure an increasingly integrated syllabus centred around the main discipline studied – economics. The economic section, while aiming to present a clear picture of the working of the economic system, is also designed to illustrate the application of economic analysis to a range of problems in the field of economic and also social policy. The sessions on statistical methods both complement and extend the economic analysis which is studied, as do the sessions on operational research techniques, game theory and decision theory, and computers. Sessions on the interpretation of company accounting and also a business game, which is played by post over a period of several weeks, contribute to the general aim of familiarising Assistant Principals with the language and methods of quantitative analysis.'[17]

A recent development in the 28-week course has been for the c.a.s. to commission short sections of the course from institutions outside the Service and to take the course to them. Institutions which have been used in this way are the University of York and the Institute of Development Studies in the University of Sussex.

Most of those attending are Assistant Principals in the age range from 23 to about 30. In addition, there are usually a few on each course from the Diplomatic Service who are sent to the Centre after completing one overseas tour, some Assistant Statisticians, one or two Inspectors of Taxes, Assistant Principals from the Government of Northern Ireland and equivalents from the Atomic Energy Authority.

In addition to this 28-week course, there have been a number of others for civil servants in their thirties and early forties (for example, courses for Principals), and these cover decision-making and management techniques, organization and staff management, economics and social administration.

There has also been some training for Assistant Secretaries. The only courses provided for them previously were of two weeks' duration and on Organization and Management, but more recently these have been developed into residential seminars lasting up to five days,

TABLE X[18]

CENTRE FOR ADMINISTRATIVE STUDIES
20-Week Course for Assistant Principals
(Number of Half-Day Sessions allocated is shown in brackets)

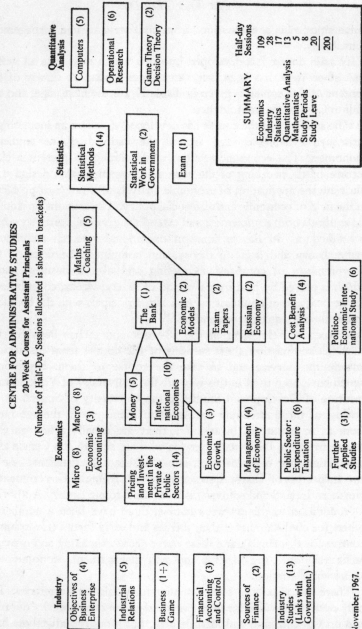

Quantitative Analysis

Computers (5)

Operational Research (6)

Game Theory Decision Theory (2)

Statistics

Statistical Methods (14)

Statistical Work in Government (2)

Exam (1)

Maths Coaching (5)

Economics

Micro (8)   Macro (8)

Economic Accounting (3)

Pricing and Investment in the Private & Public Sectors (14)

The Bank (1)

Money (5)

International Economics (10)

Economic Models (2)

Exam Papers (2)

Russian Economy (2)

Cost Benefit Analysis (4)

Economic Growth (3)

Management of Economy (4)

Public Sector: Expenditure Taxation (6)

Further Applied Studies (31)

Politico-Economic International Study (6)

Industry

Objectives of Business Enterprise (4)

Industrial Relations (5)

Business Game (1½)

Financial Accounting and Control (3)

Sources of Finance (2)

Industry Studies (Links with Government.) (13)

November 1967.

SUMMARY

	Half-day Sessions
Economics	109
Industry	28
Statistics	17
Quantitative Analysis	13
Mathematics	5
Study Periods	8
Study Leave	20
	200

each devoted to a single aspect of management and of public administration.

Whilst this training programme is in operation the Civil Service is also sending people to the Business Schools in London and Manchester as alternative institutions to Henley (where civil servants continue to attend courses). During 1965/66 the Treasury took up 22 places on these courses, and in 1966/67 it took up 35 places.[19] These courses all cover generally applicable aspects of management and administration and are therefore in some respects similar to the courses provided centrally within the Civil Service; they also act as a meeting place where senior civil servants may meet people of similar status and responsibility from other occupations.

A further opportunity for external training is provided by periods of sabbatical leave – that is, leave with pay given to selected civil servants holding, or likely to hold, positions of responsibility.[20] This may be used for advanced study (at a university or other institution either in Britain or overseas), secondment to jobs abroad or to local government, or attachment to industry. In the five years ending in 1966 the average total number of such training places taken up each year was about 12.

All these training opportunities for higher civil servants may sound interesting and valuable but the questions must be faced not only whether they are worthwhile in the sense of evaluating particular courses and particular individuals, but also whether they meet the more general requirements of the Service as a whole, for the Civil Service is not just in the 'management' business but also in the 'public' business.

The training programme may be considered in the first instance in terms of course content and whether it is relevant to the needs of the individuals involved, and there are really two aspects to be borne in mind: the subject matter and the environment of the work.

Sufficient has already been said to show that there is enormous total variety in the work performed by Administrative civil servants in the various departments of expanding government activity. In terms of subject matter there is now no less variety in government work than in work outside. Nor, does it seem, is there any effective record of the actual content of Administrative Class work at its various levels in all departments – the Service is still sufficiently departmentalised for no one to know adequately what goes on in other departments.

So there are some fields of activity which need to be understood
by civil servants in particular departments. For this purpose the
Fulton Committee suggested economic and financial, and social, as
examples of broad areas for specialisation. In addition, the scale of
work in the public service is steadily expanding and most senior
civil servants need now to know about the uses and limitations of
certain management techniques, so that they at least know when or
when not to call in specialist advisers. Because public administration
is becoming increasingly widely accepted as a term for management
activities associated with government, there is a wide variety of
specialist skills and disciplines involved in its study. These skills
and disciplines have in many cases developed outside the management
situation but have in the past twenty years been applied to that
situation more and more. The present concern with management and
training in the public service is an extension of that development to
the work of government.

In themselves, these specialist activities may be interesting and
important. They may or may not be relevant to parts of public
administration work. But one of the important consequences of this
recent interest and concern is that it has emphasised the breadth of
the subject matter of management, and also the large (often not
previously recognised) management content of much Civil Service
work. It is therefore not surprising that higher civil servants, aware of
recent management developments and the fashionable interest in
management, have appreciated opportunities through the c.a.s. and
elsewhere to find out what it is all about, and in some cases have
discovered that they have been doing it for a number of years.

There is, however, also the ecology of public administration
work. There are differences between business management and public
administration and these must also be borne in mind. For example,
public administration must be considered in relation to the political
environment, and there may be a tendency at the present time to play
down such fundamental aspects of public administration in favour of
the more fashionable management aspects. Whilst the public administrator needs to know about the area in which he works and the
inter-relations and how to integrate various disciplines in solving
management problems, he also needs to know about the social and
political environment in which he works. A significant number of the
1956 entrants (the majority of whom were history graduates) specifi-

cally said in 1966 that they would have found very helpful an early opportunity to study economics and public and political institutions.

All this may be particularly necessary for our present Administrative civil servants, bearing in mind the social and political backgrounds from which they come. New graduate entrants into the Service who have previously studied history or classics generally welcome the opportunity to learn about specialisms relevant to their everyday work. They may also be peculiarly well suited to make the best use of such opportunities – it will be remembered that one of the qualities emphasised in the recruitment process is 'mental ability'.

Whether the training opportunities at present available are the best possible is another question entirely. When it is remembered that higher civil servants may work very long hours, any opportunity to get away from the desk for a short period, in order to think and indulge in background reading, becomes valuable, even if the subject-content of particular courses could be improved (one wonders, for example, why there is so much more emphasis on economics in the c.a.s. courses for generalists than is normally given to business managers in Business School courses, and also why civil servants spend so much less time on sociological studies). The general consensus of the 1956 entrants was that almost *any* form of training would be welcomed, and they were particularly keen to take advantage of opportunities for discussions and seminars for the exchange of ideas. One of them said it would be a great help just to get away from the desk and telephone for a short spell to think in a relaxed atmosphere: 'Working in at least certain parts of the Administrative Civil Service now is like being in a treadmill . . . there is so little time in which to consider the work in a wider context.'

But even if every possible opportunity for training is accepted and developed, the Civil Service may not be reaping maximum returns if it fails to make the best use of those specialist skills and qualifications that its members already possess. This may, for example, happen through deficiencies of personnel management.

LIKES AND DISLIKES ABOUT CIVIL SERVICE WORK

Interesting information was gathered for the Fulton Committee by asking the 1956 entrants about their likes and dislikes concerning the Civil Service. The answers to 'What do you now like about the

Civil Service?' were classified by giving a weight of one to each facet mentioned (some replies gave more facets than others). The following is a list of all aspects of Civil Service work that were mentioned more than once:

Work with congenial colleagues	24
Interesting, important work, being at the centre of things	23
The intellectual quality of the work	10
Being 'in the know'; helping to shape policy	7
Working in the public service	6
Pay and/or leave	6
Absence of rat-race, presence of team spirit	6
Enables me to live where I do (London or Edinburgh)	3
Enables me to meet a lot of interesting people	2
Democracy in management (Whitleyism)	2

The answers to 'What do you now dislike about the Civil Service?' were similarly classified, and the following is a list of all aspects of Civil Service work that were mentioned more than once:

Bad man-management	19
Lack of clerical assistance	14
Bad office accommodation (e.g. sharing a room when the nature of the work is such that efficiency is seriously reduced)	10
Work interferes with my private life (usually because of long hours)	8
Doing work that I dislike (e.g. that is objectionable on political, social or philosophical grounds, or work that comes to nothing because of political pressures)	7
The cult of the amateur	6
Work below my capacity	6
Living in London	5
Anonymity	3
Lack of training	3
The Class Structure of the Service	3

Several of these categories overlap, but this cannot be helped in this type of investigation. For example, during the interview 'work below my capacity' was said to have been given either because bad management was causing the civil servants to feel that their abilities were not being fully used, or because the supporting staff was so poor (or did not exist) that the Principal had to do minor clerical duties as part of his work. Other people might simply have included these types of experience under the broad heading of 'bad management'.

Although a few of the civil servants were equipped with them, dictating machines did not seem, in 1966, to be generally available to Principals in most departments, and in many cases routine secretarial assistance did not exist either. It was common to find an ancient typewriter in a Principal's room for his own typing activities. One member of the group gratefully recalled some typing training he had received during his national service in the R.A.F.; another Principal was enrolled as an evening student in a typing class where he was the only man with about thirty women. Several Principals, recalling that there are many unfilled Principal posts at present, pointed out that this need not be so serious if better secretarial assistance was provided, as this would enable more of a Principal's time to be spent on work suited to the grade (and salaries) – typing and addressing envelopes do not need honours degrees or salaries of over £3,000.

Some of the examples of bad management (which one of the civil servants defined as 'not enough thought being given to how to *use* staff to allow them to earn their salaries') illustrate such inept staff relations that one is left wondering why there are not more resignations from the Service – though it should not be assumed that similar experiences are unknown in many business concerns. One Principal learned of his recent posting only by overhearing a telephone conversation in his Assistant Secretary's office, and the posting was never formally confirmed by the Establishments Officer. Other criticisms, based on a number of specific personal experiences which were explained to the author in confidence, showed serious lack of consideration towards staff as human beings, and some criticisms of staff management were based on incidents that had left individuals feeling very bitter, and not without good cause.

According to several of the civil servants interviewed the faults stemmed basically from the Treasury (management divisions). One or two mentioned that it had been years since they had seen or heard of a visit from a Treasury staff inspector. One or two more, with recent experience of establishments work, gave examples of how unconcerned the Treasury seemed to be about representations or suggestions made to them. Nearly all were highly critical about attitudes to training in the Civil Service, and there were examples in the sample of people with special qualifications who for no apparent good reason were being prevented from using their skills. Several of the civil servants interviewed were highly critical of what they called 'the cult of the amateur' in relation to their postings. As one of them put it: 'I have had seven jobs in my department, none lasting longer than two years, none bearing any but the most remote relation to any other; with this kind of career there is not enough scope for getting to know a job thoroughly and for acquiring enough confidence (and time) to produce new ideas and "make a difference".'

Such comments support the conclusions of the Management Group Survey, which commented unfavourably on the frequency with which Administrative civil servants are moved from one job to another. The Group found that the administrators they interviewed had been an average of 2·7 years in the job they were doing. (They had averaged a period of 3·2 years in their previous jobs and 2·8 in all their completed jobs in that Class).[21]

Several in the sample of 1956 entrants were at the time of the research, or had recently been, filling posts which did not provide a full day's work, but little notice seemed to be taken when they reported this (as they claimed to have done). On the other hand, some were required to work inordinately long hours and were complaining of the intrusion of work into their private lives. As one put it: 'In the Administrative Civil Service, if one is at all conscientious it is not a job but a way of life. It demands most of one's time and energy and this pressure is kept up so that one can see people becoming paler editions of themselves.' Another gave as a dislike 'the expectation that civil servants will work inordinate hours without regard to their family life'.

The attraction of working with congenial colleagues tended to mean two things at once. On the one hand, there is the complete absence of class distinction within the Service (to be discussed further in chapter 6). This applies not only to social class but also to the Civil Service Classes (Executive/Administrative etc.), for there is a general atmosphere of team spirit in which educational and family backgrounds are totally irrelevant. Graduates from Oxbridge and Redbrick Universities work side by side, sometimes in the same office, with those promoted from within the Service, or even those still within the Executive Class itself (in several cases Principals interviewed shared offices with civil servants in the Executive Class). What matters is that X or Y is 'a decent sort' and 'a good person to work with'. On the other hand, working with congenial colleagues often also meant having colleagues who were very intelligent and 'civilised' and of a liberal frame of mind.

THE PRESENT POSITION

The period from the mid-1960s has seen a number of developments concerning the work and training of higher civil servants, though the Fulton Report was not outstanding either as a document or for its impact on the Service. The Report followed rather than heralded changes, and had many of the defects of the amateurism it criticised. The most interesting aspect of the Report, however, is that the Committee was carried along by certain movements and changes in the Service which were already progressing with considerable speed.

Before the research done for Fulton, there was no real understanding of what higher civil servants did. Many people in the Service knew about their own work, but they were only small cogs in a large machine, and they could only think they knew what others did. Establishment Officers knew about most of the work in their own departments. The Treasury had made general statements (such as that already quoted from 'Estacode') about the policy-advising and co-ordinating content of the work of Administrative civil servants, and also maintained central records of staff work and movements – but for a number of reasons these tended to be out of date and unreliable.

There had been, of course, a number of volumes, often fascinating and valuable, of memoirs written by civil servants on retirement. However, these tended to be about what happened in a previous period, full of witty sayings and amusing anecdotes, but telling little about the work carried out and the sort of people responsible for it. This may have been caused partly by the requirements of the Service to maintain secrecy whenever possible, though it is more likely to be because the writers did not have the knowledge. C. K. Munro, for example, introduced his book by explaining: 'I have not undertaken any special research . . . but simply written from what my experience has taught me. Some of the statements which I have made, therefore, cannot be taken to apply fully to every Department of State, for things vary as between one Department and another. . . . I have made no definite attempt to explain what it is that Civil Servants in Whitehall *do*.'[22] C. H. Sisson[23] produced a character study of the permanent administration in Whitehall, and by making some European comparisons showed that he was in favour of the British system for Britain; he produced many epigrammatic sentences and wrote thoughtfully and provocatively, but his book is not outstanding for what it tells us about the work actually done by members of the Administrative Class. R. K. Kelsall's[24] valuable study concentrated primarily on selection for the higher Civil Service and related it to the social background of candidates. G. K. Fry[25] has written an outstanding essay on the development of the Administrative Class and on certain aspects of its recruitment and training, he also deals with the changing functions of government – but skilfully avoids detail about what civil servants actually do. All these (and others also) have made recommendations often fundamental for reform. Yet they are all, together with many other writings that could also be mentioned, based on only very limited knowledge. The picture that emerges is rather like the proverbial six blind men of Indostan who went to see an elephant.

Some of the most influential evidence for the Fulton Committee was produced by the Treasury both in its factual memoranda and in some of its proposals for reform. This evidence was the result of trends already being worked out inside the Service, so it was hardly surprising that a number of the Fulton recommendations were immediately acceptable to the Government.

The most important recent development is the concern to know what Administrative civil servants *do*, and the somewhat remarkable fact emerges that, with certain modifications and changes due to developing technology, what higher civil servants do now is similar in a number of important respects to what they did a hundred years ago.

Just as a hundred years ago the higher civil servant at home or in the I.C.S. had to deal with any problem within the area of his general responsibility, so today it has been justifiably said that he 'never knows what he may be in for . . .' and he 'must have a capacity to deal with all kinds of matters and situations.'[26] Just as a hundred years ago he received no formal training but rather underwent a period of initiation and socialisation, so today, if he is lucky (and most new entrants to the Administrative Class now are in this respect) he has a similar initiation, has a series of short postings to various branches in a department, and a six months' c.a.s. course concentrating primarily on economic and social administration and specialist subjects – but he receives no other basic training for the type of work he has to do.

All that has happened is that the much exalted new training courses help the higher civil servant to know more about certain background aspects of the work he may be required to do and the environment in which he works. The old distinction, between the concentration on policy decisions in the Administrative Class and slightly discretionary and routine decisions in the Executive and Clerical Classes, never really satisfied either those within the Service who were concerned with the work, or the political scientists who attempted to understand it from outside. But when government was a more restricted activity it was easier to attempt to understand the distinctions than it is today. To some extent the role of government has changed not merely from a negative to a positive state, but to something even more complicated – to a positive state that is now often not in control of its own destiny. Whilst government is concerned with the promotional aspects of what political scientists have sometimes called the positive state, civil servants have also to grapple with many influences, restrictions and controls that are complications to the work being done but are now part of the environment of government activity.

The recently introduced training courses for higher civil servants (which emphasise economics and related disciplines) help civil servants – particularly those who have graduated in 'irrelevant' subjects – to adjust more easily to situations in which they find themselves. Yet at the same time there has been no fundamental change. There has been a little easing of the blanket of secrecy about what civil servants do, so that the Fulton Committee was rather better informed than it might have been; and there has been some awareness that life is now rather different from life in previous periods due to technological advances, but that is all. There is still the emphasis in selecting recruits for the Administrative Class on a basis of intelligence, quick-wittedness, or what the Civil Service Commission has called 'mental ability'. Perhaps this is the most appropriate quality to seek if personnel are to be moved regularly from job to unrelated job at short notice. Perhaps this is the only common denominator for work in a Class

G

which is almost as various in scope as that faced by a member of the
I.C.S. a hundred years ago.

Indeed, in some respects it might still be said that there is no training.
What exists may be regarded as no more than an extension of the
socialisation process whereby the internal socialisation continues
as before, and the new courses introduce civil servants to management
techniques and procedures, and to the new role of government
(consistent with the changing pattern of life and the position of Britain
in the world). Any fundamental improvement in the training processes
to make higher civil servants better equipped for the work they have
to do must depend on more research into what Administrative civil
servants actually do, a possible re-evaluation of work in the light of
any new Class and grading structure, selection procedures based on
seeking qualities appropriate for the work to be performed, and
training courses and programmes to develop those qualities.

The essence of the problem is that public administration as a
specialist study in this country has not realised its opportunities.
For a number of reasons it has accepted artificial restrictions to its
scope and limited its area of concern primarily to a study of institutions; it has largely failed to recognise that public administration is
essentially an activity. Consequently there is inadequate basic knowledge about such aspects as the content of work performed by the
Administrative Class in the Civil Service, and it is not surprising
that there are serious inadequacies in training programmes. There is
both an insufficient understanding of the needs to be met by Civil
Service training and insufficient material to use even where the needs
to be met are understood.

This all adds to the impressive nature of recent developments, for
whilst so-called training may at present be inadequate, it has to start
somewhere and the establishment of the Civil Service College (announced by the Prime Minister in June 1968) is a laudable act of
faith – an impressive start by providing courses based on the limited
material available for training purposes and related to imperfectly
known needs.

5. The Environment for Work

'... in a Government office, as certainly as in a law-court or a laboratory, effective thinking will not be done unless adequate opportunities and motives are secured by organization during the whole working life of the appointed officials'.[1]

It is clear, from some of the likes and dislikes about the Civil Service quoted in the previous chapter, that serving civil servants may attach more importance to the conditions under which they work than to the actual content or subject matter of the work; and this is quite consistent with the results of investigations by industrial sociologists. Higher civil servants, who like to do their best whatever the particular task they find themselves doing, consider that one of the most attractive features of the Civil Service is working with congenial colleagues, and they find very frustrating those environmental features which prevent them achieving standards they set themselves. This chapter will review four such aspects of the environment in which higher civil servants find themselves working.

OFFICE SERVICES AND ACCOMMODATION

Many civil servants find tedious and frustrating what they regard as the parsimonious and short-sighted attitude in relation to the public service which results in lack of secretarial and clerical assistance, inadequate working conditions, and meanness in paying necessary personal expenses. One Principal, when asked recently what he disliked in the Civil Service, replied: 'Mainly the squalor of the practical environment – depressing offices and a lack of secretarial assistance. The latter is the thing I most resent. Like nearly all Principals I have no secretary. I waste hours trying to make telephone calls (or accepting calls I would prefer not to), looking for papers, writing papers by hand (because I cannot trust a random shorthand typist from the pool to produce an accurate first attempt and there is no time for a second), checking typing, etc. This is wholly uneconomic and a rather typical example of Treasury cheese-paring. If the Civil Service would pay to get good typing and secretarial staff I doubt whether even the typing and secretarial services would cost more, and there would be large economies in the use of staff.'[2]

The evidence of individuals has been supported and emphasised by the evidence of their staff associations to the Fulton Committee.[3] It is only a fortunate minority of staff in the Administrative Class at Principal level who even share the services of a secretary. The majority have none at all and either do their own typing or are forced to rely on the assistance of typing pools for shorthand, audio and copy typing (this can be particularly inconvenient where audio and copy typing services are decentralised and situated in towns away from London). Many, recognising from experience how disastrously unreliable such clerical assistance can be, have attempted to cut down on the amount of paper they have to deal with, and attend to it all themselves.

Such a situation is obviously a dis-service to the public, introducing avoidable inefficiency into a bureaucratic system, and false economy to a point which might make it as serious as other forms of mis-appropriation of public money.

In the first place, it is quite extraordinary that the Civil Service should recruit highly qualified staff for senior positions at salaries of over £3,000 a year, yet force them to do work appropriate for junior office staff who are paid often no more than a quarter of that salary. Whilst senior staff are so engaged they are either failing to do work they should be doing, or working inordinately long hours to cope with their duties so that they are physically fatigued when they have to make important decisions appropriate to their status in the organization. Furthermore, these conditions are prevailing at a time when the shortage of staff at Principal level has been stated by the Association of First Division Civil Servants to be as much as 10 per cent.[4] (And in the years 1954–68 the Civil Service Commission announced 983 vacancies in the Administrative Class but appointed only 826 successful candidates from its competitions)[5]. There is little doubt that the situation would be considerably eased by improving the office services available for higher civil servants, but one of the difficulties in effecting this is the way Civil Service manpower is controlled. There is great pressure from Parliament to keep down the *total* numbers in the

Service and this is reflected in the total manpower ceiling imposed on each department by the Civil Service Department. Under this system one typist equals one Permanent Secretary so the political constraint is experienced within the Service by lack of discrimination between one kind of manpower and another.

Secondly, the public are unlikely to appreciate or make allowance for the resulting inefficiencies (indeed, there is no administrative reason why such inefficiencies should be tolerated), and consequently the Civil Service tends to sink further in the estimation of the public. One Administrative Class official[6] who recently left the Service has explained that in the Home Office (not the least significant or newest government department) typing would take up to three weeks (plus another three weeks if one had second thoughts during that time). As much of the work there involves dealing with the public on sensitive matters, such delays make the work considerably more difficult than it need be (therefore, possibly requiring an official of higher status and with higher pay than would otherwise be necessary). The public, not surprisingly, attribute the delays to indecision and incompetence. It seems there *is* managerial incompetence, though not in the way popularly imagined, and often the cause is unappreciated outside the public service.

This modern variation of saving 'candle-ends' is also seen in the Civil Service regulations governing the reimbursement of claims for travelling, subsistence and removal expenses. When the Fulton Committee reported, the standard subsistence allowance for an official away from his place of duty for a period of up to ten hours was 5s. 9d. (equivalent to 29p.) and for a period exceeding ten hours 12s. 6d. (equivalent to 63p.). The principle applies with great fairness at all levels in the Service; in 1967 the annual conference of the Civil Service Clerical Association passed a resolution saying that clerical officers should get more money for using bicycles in their jobs. The cyclists are mainly Ministry of Social Security Clerical Officers who have to call on people with problems about supplementary benefits and pensions. They provide their own bicycles and receive 2d. (equivalent to 1p.) a mile up to 100 miles a month, on a scale which reduces as the mileage increases so that they can only receive the maximum of 25s. (equivalent to £1·25p.) a month if they cycle more than 301 miles.

Where cuts in the cost of the public services result in such absurd false economies they may well constitute a problem for investigation by the Estimates Committee. Yet often the reasons for them are not administrative at all but political, and must be accepted as one of the costs of our political system at its present stage of development. The public are rarely in favour of increasing taxes however good the cause, and politicians who depend on them for election tend to take note of their views – it may take what amounts to a public campaign of considerable size and intensity, such as that involved in convincing people that British attitudes to management in both public and private sectors are out of date and amateur, before money is released. And even then money may be wasted because it is often more difficult to get small sums of money for relatively minor improvements than it is to get a large sum.

The same situation can be seen in the problem of accommodation. It is quite common to find two Principals sharing a room, or a Principal sharing with two or three or more subordinates, and in some departments conditions are worse than in others. The problems of sharing are particularly difficult, for example, in the Scottish Office in Edinburgh, where most officials in the senior Executive grades and up to the middle of the Administrative Class (who earn salaries well over £3,000) do not have rooms of their own. Apart from being a serious drag on efficiency this situation gives a bad impression to people from outside who visit officials during the day; and most important, probably, is its effect on the morale of the officials concerned.

The quality of the accommodation is the responsibility of the Ministry of Public Buildings and Works which maintains the 40 million square feet of office accommodation used by government departments in the United Kingdom. Whilst the Ministry recognises[7] that the conditions of some offices are sometimes unsatisfactory and occasionally depressing, it attempts to maintain standards comparable with good employers. However, the fact remains that there is a great variety in standards. In some cases the accommodation is excellent; the present Board of Trade building, for instance, referred to by Nikolaus Pevsner as 'this monument of tiredness and distrust of the world'[8] (because it symbolised old-fashioned and uninspiring taste in architecture), has been referred to by civil servants as 'up to the highest standards one could reasonably demand ... But the comparison makes all the worse the sleaziness of St Christopher House, or the Dickensian conditions of some of the other buildings, where one may find five officials, an Assistant Principal among them, so closely jammed into a single room that their desks touch, and a coal fire in the corner.'⁹

To some extent the problems of office accommodation are insepar-ably connected with the past. The government can hardly avoid owning and continuing to use (while they remain even remotely usable) famous buildings from previous periods, but they do present problems. At the 1967 C.S.C.A. annual conference one member from the Somerset House branch of the Association explained: 'Half our members work in a building which is classified as an ancient monument. It is a very fine building in some respects, but hardly suitable for office accommodation. Some of us are lucky and work in large rooms beautifully decorated with elegant friezes and paintings. Others are unfortunate enough to be tucked away in dingy, poky rooms behind back staircases and in damp dirty vaults. Practically no improvements can be carried out without sanction from the ancient monuments section of the Ministry of Public Buildings and Works. They are usually reluctant to authorise anything in case the character of the building should suffer.'¹⁰ A Clerical Officer told Norman Fowler, Home Affairs Correspondent of *The Times*, when he talked to civil servants after the publication of the Fulton Report: 'The office where I work has tiny rickety stairs; there are cracks in the walls, and the floors slope into the centre so that you have to put books in front of the cabinets to prevent them opening. There are three pale grey walls, another in dirty yellow and it is finished off with a pink door. The ceilings are white with brown patches and the building has no fire escape.' Another civil servant told of the mouse traps that had to be put down at the old Scotland Yard building after it had been taken over by the Board of Trade.¹¹ The Association of First Division Civil Servants emphasised the same problem to the Fulton Committee when it stated that many higher civil servants occupy dirty rooms with worn, old-fashioned furniture of a standard that not only brings the Service into discredit but also induces a general air of inefficiency, and added: 'We do not share the view that austerity is a good in itself to which the public service should be conspicuously subject.'¹²

Because it is still in the nature of the Civil Service to grow, since the growth of the Service can be correlated with increasing demands for government services, many government departments are split for accommodation purposes into a number of buildings, sometimes many miles apart, and this also tends to have a serious effect on management efficiency and morale in the department (though it may appear to have relatively little effect on the conduct of the department's work – at least as far as the public is concerned). Whilst to some extent this problem is unavoidable as large departments would need vast edifices if all staff were to be accommodated together, this is nevertheless a problem which in terms of morale and its effect on efficiency has received relatively little attention. And such problems are not solved by pretending they do not exist; serious study might help to mitigate some of the unfortunate consequences.

RELATIONS BETWEEN THE CLASSES

Work in the Civil Service is organised on the basis of job classification, a concept well established in the public service. A class, when used in this technical sense in personnel management, is a group of positions sufficiently alike in their duties and responsibilities to justify common treatment in selection, pay, and other employment processes, but sufficiently different from positions of other classes to justify different treatment in one or more of these respects.[13] Classification enables work to be divided so that basically similar work can be performed by the same kind of official using the same kind of expertise. Some classes (the 'general service' classes) are large and to be found in all departments – the largest classes are the general Treasury classes such as the Administrative, Executive and Clerical; but others are small and may be found only in those departments where their particular category of work is to be found – examples of these would be the class of Actuaries (who are almost exclusively employed in the Government Actuaries Department) and the class of Inspectors of Taxes (in the Inland Revenue Department).

The classification system in the British Civil Service has its origins in the nineteenth-century division of work into two categories: intellectual, and routine. For these two types of work recruitment was linked to the educational system so that graduates were recruited for the intellectual work and non-graduates for the rest. By the middle of the twentieth century the system had become more elaborate and three general service classes had emerged, based on recruitment from the three broad levels produced by the educational system: school-leavers with 'O' levels being recruited to the Clerical Class, school-leavers with 'A' levels being recruited to the Executive Class, and graduates

being recruited to the Administrative Class. As new classes were
established the system of classification became more complicated,
though the idea throughout has been to group together for purposes
of pay, recruitment and certain other conditions of service, officials
doing broadly similar work. Critics of the Civil Service at the present
time have focused attention on the unfortunate word 'class' which
might cause confusion with social stratification and produce feelings
of inferiority (the Fulton Committee referred instead to 'occupational
groups', 'blocks of work' and 'families of jobs'); the enormous variety
of work which has sometimes to be regarded as 'similar' for classification purposes, resulting in classification imprecision; and the rigidity
of the system which makes transfer between classes difficult.

There is always the possibility of disharmony between members of
different classes – in the same way as there is the possibility of disharmony between, for example, officers and other ranks in the armed
forces. But in the British Civil Service officials generally work in a
team spirit, and this close co-operation between members of different
classes may be particularly noticeable when members of the Administrative and Executive classes have to share offices. When problems
of disharmony do arise, they are likely to be of the type that would
occur anywhere between members of different age groups looking
at problems from different points of view.

In the Civil Service at the present time the class structure has
led to attention being focused where classes are likely to work most
closely together. In practice this means considering the relationship
between on the one hand the various general classes, and on the other
hand between some of the Professional and Scientific Classes and the
general classes. As far as the higher Civil Service is concerned, attention is focused on the Administrative/Executive relationship and on
the Administrative/Professional relationship.

There are a number of positions in the Civil Service which experience has shown may be successfully filled by either senior members
of the Executive Class or members in the junior to middle grades
in the Administrative Class. One might, perhaps, have a particular
position filled at one time by a Principal and later by a Chief Executive
Officer. Such positions tend to be on the borderline of the traditional
division between Executive and Administrative Class work – highly
responsible managerial work is a good example. The difference in
the class of official chosen for such a position is likely to be one of

age and experience compared with youth and potential. A senior member of the Executive Class may know a great deal about the working of a particular department and do a good job of management by making the best use of his experience. When the same position is filled by a Principal he will have less detailed knowledge and experience but may do an equally good job by relying on other qualities he has.

Sometimes civil servants complain of the difficulties that arise between members of different classes working together as closely as they do, but such complaints tend to be of the normal variety where people of different ages and backgrounds are working together. For example, one ex-Administrative civil servant has complained: 'One can spend a lot of time and effort, given the present class structure, in skating over the thin ice of relationships with one's Executive colleagues, who often feel uneasy or inhibited about offering advice and help to this new cuckoo in the nest, predestined to status and salaries which many of them know they will never get near.'[14] On the other hand, a serving Executive civil servant has said: 'I have worked alongside scientists and engineers and there has never been a problem that has been bedevilled because we were in different classes.'[15]

More often, when Executive and Administrative officers work together, the work situation is said to be one of considerable harmony and no effort is wasted over matters of interchangeability. The Fulton proposals to replace the present terminology of job classification with a numerical scale (in which, for example, Grade V would be equivalent to Principal/Chief Executive Officer in current terminology and Grade IV equivalent to Assistant Secretary/Principal Executive Officer) may have a useful tidying-up effect, but in practice there will be no fundamental change. As one Principal recently put it, 'the barriers between the three (general) classes only exist on paper even today: and some differential for age, educational standards and aptitude at entry will still have to be maintained.'[16]

A more serious situation has arisen from the division between the Administrative Class and the Professional and Scientific Classes. Their members tend to have similar educational backgrounds and age at entry, but their career patterns are fundamentally different.

The problem as they see it has been put forcefully by the Institution of Professional Civil Servants on behalf of its members. The Institution has pointed out that the professional staff at roughly corresponding levels (in terms of age at entry and qualifications) is about the same in total number as the Administrative and Executive staff, but has added that thirty-three out of the thirty-six posts at Permanent Secretary level are held by members of the Administrative Class.[17] It has also argued that at all levels the Works Group of Professional and Scientific Officer Classes have earnings and prospects well below those of the Administrative Class. The essence of the I.P.C.S. case is that the relationship between the 'specialist' classes and the general Administrative and Executive Classes 'has been unsatisfactory'. 'In some cases there has been undue interference by Administrative and Executive staff with the work of Professional and Technical staff. In others, the role allotted to Administrative staff is not conducive to harmonious relationships.'[18] It has been argued that the professionals should be given more administrative responsibilities and control over the work on which they are engaged, and there should be greater ease of transfer from the professional to the general classes.[19]

Apart from the expressed desire for equality of status and more pay, it is not clear that professionals do so generally desire to become administrators, or have the necessary qualities, though there are indeed few opportunities for re-training or re-classification. However, the administrative content of Professional Class work may be as under-appreciated as the managerial content of Administrative Class work: no adequate research has been done to examine either situation.

The average direct entrant to the Administrative Class has in the past had the prospect of earning more both at an earlier age and in total than his contemporaries in the professional classes. But whilst their age at entry and academic qualifications may be similar, the selection process is different. Whereas the selection process for the Administrative Class attempts to assess qualities other than the purely academic, entrants to, for example, the Scientific Officer Class are judged primarily on their ability to undertake particular scientific work. But there is nothing to prevent a suitably qualified scientist from competing for admission to the Administrative Class if he wished, and on the same conditions as apply to other applicants.

The Social Survey of the Civil Service carried out for the Fulton Committee found that there were certain measurable differences between members of the Administrative Class and other higher classes in the Service, as well as between the Administrative Class and top managers in industry and commerce. The typical member of the Administrative Class is aged forty-six (between thirty-nine and forty in the lower grades and just under fifty in the upper grades).[20] According to A. H. Halsey and I. M. Crewe they are therefore younger than men who reach comparable positions in British industry and commerce and they found that only 35 per cent of the Administrative Class are over fifty compared with 56 per cent of directors and 46 per cent of top managers. The Administrative Class is still the youngest of the higher classes, distinctly so compared with the Legal Class and Professional Works Group.[21]

The Social Survey also found differences between the educational backgrounds of members of the higher classes. Details of the types of school attended and proportions of graduates in the higher classes are shown in Table XI.

TABLE XI[22]

SCHOOL ATTENDED AND PROPORTION OF GRADUATES
OF HIGHER CLASSES IN THE CIVIL SERVICE

School attended	Administrative Class	Legal Class	Professional Works Group	Experimental Officer Class	Scientific Officer Class
L.E.A.					
Grammar	40%	22%	33%	54%	57%
Direct Grant	19%	11%	13%	12%	15%
Public School	36%	54%	19%	8%	20%
Other	5%	13%	35%	26%	8%
Total	100%	100%	100%	100%	100%
Proportion of Graduates	76%	67%	18%	18%	92%

Over half the graduates in the Administrative and Scientific Officer Classes have a first or upper second-class honours degree (at least a third have a first), but only a fifth have a lower second or below. The proportions are reversed for the other three graduate classes of whom a fifth or less have a first or upper second class degree and only half have lower seconds or below (over half the Legal Class have lower second-class degrees or below – with 39 per cent of them falling into the latter category). Of the graduate members of the Administrative Class, 64 per cent came from Oxbridge, compared with 50 per cent in the Legal Class, 15 per cent in the Professional Works Group, 16 per cent in the Scientific Officer Class and 8 per cent in the Experimental Officer Class.[23]

It may be argued that knowledge of what administrators actually do is still very limited, but there is evidence to suggest that one of the most important characteristics of an Administrative civil servant, after he has been in the Service for a few years, is his increasing appreciation of the political environment and content of his work – an appreciation which is unlikely to be gained to the same extent by a specialist who is employed to perform quite different functions, and who tends to be shielded from the peculiar frustrations encountered when dealing with politicians and the politically active public. The qualities demanded by work in various classes of the higher Civil Service may therefore be distinctly narrower and potentially more highly sophisticated than in apparently comparable posts in other parts of the public service (for example, in local government chief officers are often specialists who find themselves in primarily administrative posts which bring them into contact with councillors but in such a way that they may also be exercising – to a certain extent – their specialist training).

Furthermore, there is evidence to suggest that the majority of specialists in the Civil Service do not wish to become administrators. Sir Richard Way, then Permanent Secretary, Ministry of Aviation, in evidence to the Estimates Committee in 1965, said that most scientists hate the idea of becoming administrators. Although one-third of his Assistant Secretaries and one-third of his Principals had science degrees, the Ministry was so anxious to get as many scientists as possible into the Administrative Class that every year it reviewed its Scientific Officers with a view to transferring them to the Administrative Class if they wished: the procedure was to invite interested scientists to submit applications for transfer. Although the number of Principal Scientific Officers alone was 467 in 1955 (there were also large numbers of Senior Scientific Officers and Scientific Officers), only 25 applied; 23 applied in 1957; 22 applied in 1959; and 4 applied in 1961.[24]

Sir Richard Way's evidence suggested that a significant proportion of the administrators in his department were highly qualified in the subject matter of their specialist field of administration and were far from being the out-of-touch amateurs of the popular image. Similar evidence was given by Sir Eric Roll, then Permanent Under-Secretary of State, Department of Economic Affairs. He told the Committee that 43 per cent of his Administrative staff (Administrative, not Professional economic staff) had degrees or qualifications in economics and about half that number had first-class honours degrees.[25] Such proportions of Administrative staff, highly qualified in the specialist discipline with which they are involved, may well aid good communications because of their familiarity with technical terms and attitudes of mind of the specialists; they may also contribute to the team spirit which is sometimes said to exist between civil servants from different classes. It was not surprising in these circumstances that Sir Richard Way was able to tell the Estimates Committee that at the higher ranks the distinction between scientists and administrators 'just does not exist'.[26] It seems that where a particular specialist does not get on well with an Administrator the reason is quite likely to be, as Dale suggested, natural incompatibility: and 'the notion that the administrators despise or disregard the technical men as such is pure nonsense'.[27]

THE DEPARTMENTS AND THE ADMINISTRATIVE PROCESS

Although (or because) civil servants know very little of the detailed work of other departments they nevertheless tend to develop a loyalty to the department where they belong, and to accumulate impressions from its point of view on what they feel is done elsewhere. Each department has its own atmosphere and ways of working; it also has what Lord Bridges has called a 'departmental point of view'.[28] According to Bridges the departmental philosophy is the result of the slow accumulation of experience over the years, an institutional but specialised knowledge of the subjects handled. 'It is quite different from anything which any single man or woman could have produced; it is less logical but wiser and more comprehensive: above all, it is something which works, and which works better than anything else so far produced'.[29]

This appreciation of departmental philosophy may in some respects be laudable; but it may also be a sign of a serious administrative deficiency. It may be an advantage to have it as a useful guide to decision-making, a sort of backcloth of consensus to which individuals can turn in time of perplexity; but on the other hand it may reflect a somewhat complacent pragmatism by saying it is good because it works better than anything else produced, without considering the precious few alternatives to established departmental procedures and attitudes.

The departmental view has its origin in the post entry socialisation experienced by new recruits. This is the procedure, already discussed in Chapter 4, whereby officials in the Administrative class (and often in other general classes, too) change their jobs as soon as they are beginning to master them. They generally expect to be moved every two or three years, but fairly regular moves at intervals of eighteen months are not unknown. The idea behind this procedure is, according to Bridges, to induce a wider outlook. 'The first time a man is told to change from work he has mastered to a new job, he may feel that the special knowledge he has acquired is being wasted. He may grudge the labour of mastering a new subject and may even wonder whether he will be equally successful at it. But when a man has done five jobs in fifteen years and has done them all with a measure of success, he is afraid of nothing and welcomes change.'[30]

No adequate research has been carried out to examine the validity and possible significance of Bridges' astute observations; it would be valuable to know what influence this procedure has on the minds of individual administrators and their attitudes to their work. It may have an effect similar to that sometimes noticeable in the armed forces where an individual is 'disciplined' (that is, made to conform to a general pattern which makes him a slave to the system and crushes what is thought to be wasteful originality). Although many higher civil servants do in fact originate work, even of a policy nature, the work so initiated is likely to have, as a result, a distinctive flavour; and since the relationship between politicians and the official bureaucracy is so finely balanced in our political system the results may not all be to the disadvantage of the individual citizen.

There is little doubt that departmental attitudes and views do exist both within the department and in relation to other departments. During the survey for 'Profile of a Profession' two of these general attitudes were expressed by a number of the civil servants questioned. One that was typical and summarised many officials' views of their own departments was, 'I like my department because of the nature of the work, friendly and relaxed atmosphere, and it is the devil I know'. The civil servants also frequently expressed opinions (though, as they emphasised themselves, based on very slender evidence) about other departments. The one most frequently mentioned concerned the Treasury: 'People who get sent to the Treasury seem to be the "cream" and therefore of much greater ability', 'The Treasury and D.E.A. are attractive because they are the centre of policy formation'. Other sentiments expressed, all of which are relevant to this aspect of the study, were: 'I would find unattractive any department without a history or without a future (such as the Department of Land and Natural Resources or the Colonial Office)', 'The Commonwealth Relations Office is unattractive because it has lost an Empire and not yet found a role – it is rather like looking after the Emperor's new clothes', 'What would make a department "attractive" overall would be a good Permanent Secretary and other senior staff, a good prevailing attitude to the public and to the staff, sensitively conceived staff training and staff administration, and adequate office services'.

Given the system that exists, considerable disturbance and serious damage to the efficient performance of public business may be caused by redistributing work between various departments. The effect on work unaccomplished is soon reflected in the heavy in-trays, but the effect on morale and the will to get things done is less clearly seen. Again, no adequate research is known to have been done on this, yet some government business is transferred from department to department with frightening lack of concern. Civil Aviation, for example, was transferred in 1945, 1953, 1959 and 1966. And when, in 1966, the change took place which created the Ministry of Social Security considerable ill-feeling was later publicly expressed by some officials: the clerical staff, for example, first heard from a television broadcast in 1966 of the plan to reorganise the Ministry of Pensions and National Insurance and the National Assistance Board, and union representatives were still unable to get a definite date for the proposed merger as late as May, 1966, though the New Ministry came into being on 8th August. Because the change was made at a time of abnormally heavy work in the department (the Government had simultaneously introduced earnings-related supplements and a revised scale of payments for supplementary benefits) the result was to introduce almost continuous overtime at the Ministry and serious discontent among the staff.[31]

The departmental philosophy is also stimulated by administrative processes common in the Service, the essence of which has been aptly expressed by saying that decisions are not made, they emerge.[32] The procedure on any particular important issue is for a relatively junior official – perhaps an Assistant Principal, a Principal, or a senior member of the Executive Class – to gather relevant details, often from earlier files, write a draft or minute on the particular problem, and pass it to his superior who considers it, amends it if necessary, and adds his own comments before passing it higher. In this way it is very difficult to say who, in the last resort, made the most influential contribution to the decision. Few decisions are made by individuals on their own, they are more likely to be made by groups of people. Much also depends on the facts of the case, and when all the relevant facts are collected and analysed the decision itself may be quite obvious. Or sufficient time may have passed to alter entirely the situation, and the decision may emerge as the inevitable solution. Whatever the process in an individual instance, the contributions to decision-making may be so various that from the administrative point of view it may be good fortune that the doctrine of ministerial responsibility exists in the British political system. The doctrine enables civil servants to maintain public silence, and perhaps pretend they have no views of their own. In practice they are not the *éminences grises* of popular imagination, hiding behind slightly deprecating references to their political masters, but human beings maintaining a judicial silence in a delicate political situation where none has the complete answer to any specific problem.

Whether this situation is good or bad is not a concern of this study. The fact is that it exists, and it is necessary to understand how it works, its advantages and disadvantages, and its effects on individuals in the political, as well as the administrative, system before any alternative is seriously advocated.

THE IMAGE OF THE CIVIL SERVICE

H. E. Dale, writing in the 1930s, observed that in the inter-war period the tone of writers when describing the official was very different from that before the First World War. He considered that

H

the official had become, if not beloved, at least respected and almost praised.[33] In support of his view Dale referred to the character Sir Walter Bullivant in the novels by John Buchan, and to the civil servant described by W. L. George: 'That man of oil, steel and silk, capable of every delay and grace, suggestive of every sympathy and capable of none; incapable of a lie, always capable of an evasion; determined in public utility, yet not blind to private advancement, singularly addicted to justice, yet unable to suffer mercy; not a man but a theorem, a diagram, a syllogism.'[34]

Thirty years later and after another World War (which must have influenced the image of the Civil Service at least as much as the First World War, for many more people were enabled temporarily to sample the official life) there has been a change again. Anthony Sampson records R. A. Butler as saying, about higher civil servants: 'They have silky minds, they've Rolls-Royce minds. In fact, the Civil Service is a bit like a Rolls-Royce – you know it's the best machine in the world, but you're not quite sure what to do with it. I think it's a bit too smooth: it needs *rubbing up* a bit.'[35] Sampson, however, has given a picture which is perhaps more typical of the contemporary image of higher civil servants: they are highly educated amateurs. In 1957 the novelist C. P. Snow described the 'corridors of power':

'The most characteristic picture of modern power is nothing at all sinister. It is no more or less remarkable than an office – I mean, an office building. Office buildings are much the same all over the world. Down the corridor of one of these offices, of any of them, a man is walking briskly. He is carrying a folder of papers. He is middle-aged and well-preserved, muscular and active. He is not a great tycoon but he is well above the middle of his particular ladder. He meets someone in the corridor not unlike himself. They are talking business. They are not intriguing. One of them says: "This is going to be a difficult one" – meaning a question on which, in a few minutes, they are going to take different sides. They are off to a meeting of a dozen similar bosses. They will be at it for hours. This is the face of power in a society like ours.'[36]

But in 1964, C. P. Snow advanced his image by describing Sir Hector Rose, in his novel *Corridors of Power*, as an 'old fashioned civil servant . . . exuding the old fashioned amateur air'.[37] Although no adequate research has been done into it, the general image of the Civil Service seems to have changed, and particularly the higher Civil

Service as part of it. Sampson's chapter on the Civil Service seems an accurate record of the post-Second World War structure (though the reaction to Chapter One of the Fulton Report, with its reference to the philosophy of the amateur being 'obsolete at all levels and in all parts of the service'[38] may prove a signal for further change).

There may be a number of reasons for this change. Among them, the increased spending on advertising for recruitment, together with all the other efforts recently made by the Civil Service Commission to compete with industrial recruitment schemes. There has been a slight relaxation in allowing publicity – Sir William Armstrong, Head of the Civil Service, has made some highly successful television appearances. There has also been increased mobility into and out of the Service and a change in the academic attitude to the study of public administration, which has shifted the emphasis from a study of institutions to a study of management problems in the public service. And the 1960s has been a period for analysis of what's wrong with Britain.[39] Although no one can be sure whether the image of the higher Civil Service *is* important, there is little doubt that it *could* be important for a number of reasons.

When asked whether they thought people generally in this country have a true image of what the higher Civil Service is like, the 1956 direct entrants into the Administrative Class who were interviewed for 'Profile of a Profession' fell into two distinct groups. On the one hand there were about half who thought that people generally had no idea what Administrative civil servants did and it did not really matter; one of this group added 'there would be something wrong with a country with an excessive admiration for its Civil Service'.

The other half also thought most people had no idea what higher civil servants did but thought it did matter, partly because the bad image had a poor effect on morale in the Service and partly because it had a disastrous effect on recruiting. One said: 'When I told a relative, who is a local businessman and has a pathological hatred of governments and officials, that I was to enter the Service, he was genuinely distressed because he thought good material was going to waste. I met this attitude elsewhere among friends, relatives and even other undergraduates who preferred teaching and industry to the Civil Service.'

When asked for a remedy for this situation, a very large majority of the group suggested less anonymity. 'Civil servants have taken the cult of anonymity too far . . . it would do the image of the Civil Service a lot of good if, for example, Permanent Secretaries appeared on television from time to time (it would also, I suspect, do the civil servants a lot of good).' Many suggested civil servants explaining, on television or radio, details of policies that had been decided, taking part in documentaries dealing with particular problems which civil servants are trying to solve, more participation in university seminars by senior civil servants, and even a television version of the Public Accounts Committee and the Estimates Committee. All these suggestions could do a good deal for the Service and could be arranged without conflicting with Ministerial responsibility (in any case there would be no obligation for particular civil servants to do any of these things, but the argument was that they should be able to do so if they are willing).

When the 1956 entrants were asked to give a description of the typical Administrative civil servant, quite a large proportion found this impossible, often because, as they put it, there are so many exceptions. Others explained that an administrative civil servant 'cannot be type-cast [*sic*], what emerges in an attempt to do so is either an ideal or platitudes', and 'I know so many administrators so well that it is their differences rather than their similarities that have left their impression . . . you have a general idea about things you don't know well; for example, I have a general idea about stock-brokers'.

On the other hand, those who attempted the description tended to fall between giving a useless factual description (such as 'educated at Oxbridge, with three children, works long hours often taking work home, middle-aged etc.') and describing what appeared to them as being general characteristics ('a bit stuffy and short on ideas', 'generally unworldly', 'nearly all have too little money, inclination or time left to be anything but a little dull', 'an idealist with his feet on the ground', 'a little cynical, or at any rate sceptical, not a particularly colourful personality', 'civilised in general approach, but not necessarily cultured because most have no time').

They tended to find it much easier to say whether they considered themselves to be typical members of the Administrative Civil Service. Nineteen out of thirty-two felt they were more or less typical and only ten thought they were definitely not typical.

The image of the higher Civil Service (whatever it is) may be of considerable importance for at least three reasons.

First, the image may be important for recruiting good staff. Three out of the thirty-two 1956 entrants interviewed specifically said they took the Civil Service examination to spite their university careers advisers who had told them they did not stand much chance as they had not been to Oxbridge (and if one in eleven of the *successful* candidates entered in this frame of mind, one wonders how many more potential candidates have been successfully dissuaded from entering the competition).

Sir Lawrence Helsby, then Head of the Civil Service, told the Estimates Committee in 1965 of the opinion of university staff; 'that the Service depends for its attraction to young men on qualities other than those that can be shown in a sophisticated piece of advertising. They respect the integrity, for instance, of the Service, they respect the element of public service which is involved in joining',[40] but he added that these qualities looked a little different when stated in an advertisement however skilfully it is done.[41] The Service has greatly increased its expenditure on advertising – for example, in 1964–65 the estimate was almost eight times that of 1959–60,[42] and although Sir George Abell, then First Civil Service Commissioner, told the Estimates Committee that there was no clear correlation between increased spending and recruitment, he also told them, 'it has made the departments happier and has certainly improved the image of the Civil Service in a much needed direction'.[43] However, since the publication of the Report from the Estimates Committee, there has been a marked change in the entry for the open competition for the Administrative Class: in 1965 there were more entrants from other universities than from Oxbridge, and by 1968 64·9 per cent of the applicants came from universities other than Oxford and Cambridge. In 1968 the success rate had also changed so that 41 per cent of the successful candidates came from such other universities. This suggests that more accurate knowledge about the Service may help combat prejudice and encourage undergraduates more generally to consider it seriously as a possible career.

Secondly, the image may be important for morale. Put simply, people who work long hours in often unattractive employment conditions can withstand only a certain amount of publicity that they are incompetent amateurs before their work performance is affected.

This situation may also be aggravated by civil servants being unable to leave the Service easily if they desire (the non-contributory pension scheme has been referred to as 'a dictatorial attempt to tie employees for life'.[44])

Thirdly, the changed image, with a Civil Service now wishing to appear less amateur, more open, and less unnecessarily restricted by a rigorous and indiscriminate application of the Official Secrets Act, is unlikely to leave unaffected the day-to-day working of officials. It is likely, for example, to affect the attitudes of civil servants to their duties and responsibilities; it could result in important changes in the relationship between civil servants and the public; and most important of all, it is likely to have a significant effect on the relationship between politicians and civil servants in a political system where the doctrine of ministerial responsibility has traditionally been regarded as a pillar.

6. Life outside the Office

'. . . However able our officials are, and however varied their origin, the danger of the narrowness and rigidity which has hitherto so generally resulted from official life would still remain, and must be guarded against by every kind of encouragement to free intellectual development.'[1]

Plato considered that in his commonwealth the manner of life of his guardians – how they should live and be housed – was important for the greatest possible happiness of the community as a whole. Similarly, in modern Britain, it is important to know about the manner of private life of higher civil servants in order to understand officials as people, and to appreciate their roles in the community. It may not be possible to understand how they behave in the office unless they are also considered as individuals away from their offices; and the high official would be a failure if he were inhuman.

Although the time they can devote to their families and other interests may have to be squeezed into what is left after the demands of work are met, there are aspects of their private lives which are in some respects different from those of non-officials in our society. To say, as some do, that a civil servant is only half a citizen, is a crude summary of the situation, yet it contains an easily misunderstood element of truth.

STYLE OF PRIVATE LIFE

During the cohort study of 1956 entrants to the Administrative Class it was found that very few Administrative civil servants live in central London (within about five miles of Whitehall). In fact, only four out of twenty-six lived in the centre and of those four, two had substantial private incomes and the other two were unlikely to live there for long. The majority lived either in Outer London (elsewhere within the London postal area), or in the dormitory suburbs beyond.

This can be very important for its effect on their private lives. If, for example, a Private Secretary, who may expect to work a regular sixty-hour week, lives in, say, Sevenoaks, then he may reasonably expect to spend $1\frac{1}{2}$ hours each way travelling to and from the office daily – a total travelling time of fifteen hours in a five-day week: in effect, an additional fifteen hours taken up by work, and above that which may be spent by his Minister who tends, at least during the week when Parliament is sitting, to stay in the centre of London. He may choose to live where he does because he cannot afford to live in central London, and may choose a Kentish suburb because it is a pleasant place to live, his family likes it, there are good schools, or for any of a number of other reasons. But it does mean that the amount of time he can spend with his family is seriously restricted and he has little opportunity to take part in many organised leisure-time activities. Higher civil servants may therefore have restrictions on their private lives similar to those experienced by large numbers of people belonging to other occupational groups both within and outside the Service. But an interesting difference is the very high proportion of the Administrative Class who work in central London: the Social Survey of the Civil Service found that 87 per cent of the Administrative Class work in central London (within four miles of Charing Cross), 7 per cent work in Scotland and 5 per cent work in the rest of England and Wales. It is, in fact, the highest proportion in London of any Civil Service Class – 78 per cent of the Legal Class work in central London but only 39 per cent of the Professional Works Group.[2] It is also interesting that this represents an even greater metropolitan concentration than among United States 'programme managers' of whom 82 per cent work in Washington.[3]

Only four of the thirty-five 1956 entrants who completed the questionnaire in 1966 were members of a London Club (two belonged to the Oxford and Cambridge University, one to the Travellers' and one to the United University) but two of the four were in the Scottish Department and therefore resident in Edinburgh. These figures are somewhat different from the impression given by Dale in the 1930s who, writing of higher civil servants (though it must be remembered that he regarded only civil servants *above* the grade of Principal as falling within this scope) said that 'nearly all belong to one (rarely to two) of six of the great clubs within easy reach of Whitehall – the Athenaeum, the Travellers', the Reform, the Union, the United

University, and the Oxford and Cambridge'.[4] Indeed, some of the 1956 entrants found it almost amusing that they should be seriously asked about membership of London Clubs. This lack of interest in belonging to clubs may be partly caused by general changes in the mode of life (such as higher civil servants living now in the outer suburbs instead of in central London) and partly also by changing fashions – if belonging to a London Club is a fashion.

Eighteen of the group were regular church-goers (fifteen Church of England, two non-conformist and one Roman Catholic). Six were members of local Residents' Associations. Apart from such memberships they tended to belong to a not surprising cross-section of local history societies, music societies, theatre clubs, etc. Two had rather unusual club memberships – one belonged to ten ornithological societies and another belonged to seven climbing and ski clubs.

Several, when asked whether there were any other associations they would like to belong to, said they would like to belong to more clubs and associations (they usually mentioned cultural or benevolent associations) but added that this was impossible because they had not the time, or the demands of their work made it impossible. Only one, in answer to that question, specifically mentioned that he would like to belong to 'one or two London Clubs'.

Perhaps it was not surprising that the number of clubs and associations they belonged to was not so large as the numbers they belonged to when at university. Clearly, this was a reflection of their different style of life, and people tend to join in more activities at university than they are able to keep up when they leave. But the comments of the civil servants suggested that there was more to it than just that difference.

People who daily spend about nine hours in a government office, doing important work against considerable pressure of time, are likely to be physically and mentally fatigued when they leave the office. But when, in addition, they may have to spend a further two or three hours travelling to and from work, they are more or less completely exhausted, and have little inclination towards leisure activities. A significant proportion of the 1956 entrants specifically said they wanted to do much more with their leisure time, though it should also, perhaps, be admitted that these were the people who tended already to be the most active joiners. As one of them put it: 'I do not have much leisure time. I normally work late, come home tired, have dinner and that's that. I used to have a wide spread of interests (the list on my form for entry into the Civil Service was impressive) and a big circle of friends, but work has eaten into both ... I feel like a mole nowadays.' Another simply explained: 'No leisure ... Go once weekly to theatre or cinema and occasionally entertain.'

Apart from memberships of clubs and associations, the 1956 group followed a wide and unclassifiable field of other interests and spare-time activities. Some examples will illustrate this: model making; historical research and writing articles for learned journals; music (e.g. membership of a choir or orchestra); university teaching in the evenings; writing books on mountaineering and skiing (author of the Penguin Handbook *Mountaineering*). In addition, most of them mentioned interests associated with the home, garden, motoring, sport, reading, etc. If one can legitimately generalise about this information, most of the Principals seemed to enjoy a fairly balanced mixture of indoor and outdoor, active and passive, creative and receptive activities.

The research for the Social Survey of the Civil Service drew attention to an interesting, though not entirely unexpected, contrast between the club and association memberships of members of the Administrative Class and members of the Scientific Officer Class and Professional Works Group. The latter two groups belong in large numbers to professional associations which bring them into contact with people working in similar occupations outside the Civil Service. Very few in the Administrative Class are members of such professional associations connected with their work.[5]

The survey for 'Profile of a Profession' found that, generally speaking, higher civil servants like to meet people and go to social gatherings; less than a quarter of those surveyed said they preferred not to. But a significant proportion made qualifications which suggest they prefer small rather than large gatherings ('it depends very much on the kind of people and social gatherings') and several specifically said they liked to meet people 'anywhere other than at sherry parties and cocktail parties'.

One of the group said she liked to meet people and go to social gatherings but she has now little opportunity to do so; and another, who had left the Civil Service, said that he was friendly with less people while he was a civil servant than he had been since leaving, and this was primarily because of the demands of the Service which affected his private life (the same person also said that he had been more regular in church attendance since leaving the Service).

They said they were quite often asked by their friends for advice or comments about social or political matters; this is because friends know they are civil servants and it is generally believed that the work they do gives them more insight into social and political problems. One of them added, however, that whilst civil servants are more likely to be asked for opinions and advice 'people play fair and do not expect more than a certain amount of political comment'.

It was interesting also to discover from the survey for 'Profile of a Profession' which newspapers and periodicals were read regularly by the thirty-five people in the sample ('regularly' means for daily newspapers at least three times a week, and for Sunday newspapers and other weeklies it means at least once every two weeks). Table XII gives the details.

Research was also conducted on this matter for the Social Survey of the Civil Service. It found that members of the Administrative and Legal Classes are the most regular readers of 'serious' daily newspapers in the order: *The Times*, *The Guardian*, *The Daily Telegraph*. Among the Scientific Officer Class and Professional Works Group and the intermediate classes, *The Daily Telegraph* is the most popular daily followed by *The Times*. Of Sunday newspapers, *The Observer* is the most popular among the Administrative and Scientific Officer Class, followed by *The Sunday Times* and the *Sunday Express*. The other higher and intermediate classes also most frequently read these three newspapers but in a different order of preference, reversed in the case of the Professional Works Group and Executive Class. *The Economist* is the most popular periodical for the Administrative, Legal, Scientific Officer and Executive Classes and the Professional Works Group.[6]

Although it may still be possible to find a higher civil servant whose work does not stretch him to capacity, this is now very rare – the position has completely changed since the inter-war period (as it was then said to have changed since the period before the First World War). The official life is now very different and considerably more hectic than in the past. Similarly with the private lives of officials. Dale was able to say of their private lives, 'they belong to one or more of the great clubs, if married they inhabit houses which require at least two domestic servants, they play golf and lawn tennis . . . In

TABLE XII

NEWSPAPERS AND PERIODICALS READ REGULARLY BY
A GROUP OF ADMINISTRATIVE CIVIL SERVANTS

Daily Newspaper		Sunday Newspaper	
The Times	23	The Observer	23
The Guardian	15	The Sunday Times	17
Financial Times	8	Sunday Telegraph	2
Daily Telegraph	4	Sunday Express	2
Scotsman	3	None	4
Glasgow Herald	2		
Daily Mirror	2		
Daily Mail	1		
Daily Express	1		
None	2*		

* The two who claimed not to read a daily newspaper were specially questioned
about this and confirmed their answers.

Weekly periodicals		In addition the following were
Economist	21	read regularly by one person
New Society	10	in the sample
New Statesman	9	Aeroplane
Spectator	5	Architectural Journal
Times Literary Supp.	5	British Medical Journal
Listener	4	Electrical Times
New Scientist	3	Engineer
Statist	2	Financial Mail
Times Educational Supp.	2	Motor Cycle
Country Life	2	Newsweek
Local Newspaper (various)	3	New Yorker
Church Newspaper (various)	2	Pulse
None	4	Punch
		Time
		West Africa
		Woman's Mirror

London, high officials are to be found mostly in Chelsea, Kensington,
Campden Hill, and Bayswater – the districts of the great class which
is prosperous without being rich . . .'.[7] Today, the situation has changed
considerably and it may now be more accurate to say of the private life
of a higher civil servant: 'Out of the office he is simply one of the

struggling middle class, having to do his own washing-up and be his own handy-man.'[8]

POLITICAL ATTITUDES

Civil servants do not actively engage in party politics; in this sense their lives as citizens may therefore be thought to be restricted. In practice, however, this is not usually considered a serious restriction on their private lives because they tend not to have burning desires to write to newspapers or become political leaders either nationally or locally (in this, as in other respects also, they are like a lot of people not in the Civil Service). If they had wanted to do such things they would not have remained in established, senior positions in the Service.

Very little is known of the political attitudes of civil servants. Dale, in the 1930s, gave his impression of their general views as being 'Left Centre' and he thought that if a poll had been taken half would at that time have voted Liberal.[9] But it would be quite wrong for any official body even to attempt, in the British situation, to find out how a higher civil servant voted; it would be regarded as a completely unjustifiable intrusion into their private lives.

At the same time, without some information about this facet of his character as a man, a citizen, a voter, only a very partial understanding of the high official can be gained. This has not, of course, prevented recommendations being made to such bodies as the Fulton Committee[10] on this subject; but any such recommendations must be founded at best on inspired guesswork, and more often on potentially dangerous naïveté and ignorance.

It was with considerable hesitancy that this subject was raised with civil servants during the survey for 'Profile of a Profession'. Of course, it had been made perfectly clear that there was no obligation to answer any of the questions put to them as part of the research, and this was particularly stressed in relation to the questions about politics. However, members of the group were usually very pleased to speak about their attitudes to party politics – indeed many of them welcomed the opportunity to explain how they felt about such matters.

Each was asked how he voted at the last general election (1966). None preferred not to answer, and the results were as follows:

Labour	17
Conservative	6
Liberal	4
Scottish Nationalist	1
Did not vote	2

This is just the sort of distribution a psephologist would have expected from a sample of that age group, with that educational background, at that particular election. There was nothing exceptional about the distribution, it seemed perfectly normal. However, only eight out of the thirty said they consistently voted for the same party at elections and twenty claimed (some forcefully) to be floating voters. Many answered the question about how they voted only on condition that their reasons or general views about politicians were also considered. The reasons tended to show that they did not really align themselves with the party for which they voted, but instead had voted for the man, or had some other personal reason for voting in a particular way. They were also asked their views of the political attitudes of people in the Administrative Civil Service generally, and the replies showed that twelve people felt that Administrative civil servants tended to be more to the left of centre whereas only six felt that Administrative civil servants tended to be more to the right of centre (twelve had no views). Perhaps the most useful information that emerged from discussing political views were the comments which the civil servants made. They included:

'There is a marked lack of political enthusiasm in the Civil Service';
'Civil servants tend to admire politicians who are business-like rather than amateur; this is irrespective of party';
'Party politics is not discussed';
'The efficiency of a Government in office tends to influence one's views . . . in many cases it is difficult to differentiate between parties – they all consist of politicians';
'The trouble with politicians is that they don't make decisions on the facts of the case . . . enthusiasm for a new administration was very noticeable in the early days of the Labour Government, but this may be waning now';
'Our department has been considerably affected by the Government's

programme, and their plans are poorly thought of, so that whereas two years ago probably up to 60 per cent of the Administrative civil servants here may have favoured Labour, I think there would be fewer now';

'People don't really talk about party politics in the office';

'I suppose I am really an anarchist';

'However favourable to one party a civil servant is, he soon becomes aware of the ineptitudes of any party . . . we see the merits and de-merits of any particular policy';

'If you are emotionally concerned about party politics you don't become a civil servant';

'Civil servants don't often discuss their party political views among themselves';

'Party loyalties are not very noticeable – they are irrelevant when you are close to the working of government';

'I have no time for politicians';

'A characteristic of civil servants is that they try not to do good for people against their wishes . . . I doubt whether senior civil servants crystallise their political opinions';

'I don't discuss these matters with my colleagues';

'At a recent election I voted Communist by mistake (and later discovered that the Communist candidate received only four votes), this happened because I had decided I did not wish to vote for either the Labour or the Conservative candidate and assumed the third candidate on the ballot paper was the Liberal';

'I can't remember how I voted last time';

'Up to a year ago many people in the Civil Service were clearly to the left of centre, but there is now a disenchantment with the present Government . . . though they [the civil servants] are probably still rather left of centre';

'Many civil servants will not have strong feelings about whether, for example, a particular industry should be nationalised, but they *are* keen to ensure that what is to be done is done efficiently.'

These views are very valuable and most revealing. They help explain a great deal that people have felt they knew in the past, but did not fully understand. The comments seem particularly important and relevant for this present study.

First, it should not be thought that Administrative civil servants are spineless nonentities as far as politics is concerned. On the contrary, there is considerable evidence to suggest otherwise. On particular *issues* they often have strong views – the following three comments also made during the interviews for 'Profile of a Profession' illustrate this well: 'I find the Ministry of Overseas Development most attractive because it is tackling the biggest problem facing the world, that of world poverty'; 'The Ministry of Overseas Development is unattractive because it has been created to pursue a fatuous and misguided policy'; 'I have political objections to its work – I don't believe in giving money to ungrateful people' (none of the officials who made these comments in fact work for that Ministry). Another member of the group, in answer to the question 'What particularly attracted you to the Civil Service?' replied: 'My family were strongly anti-bureaucratic and at the time I joined the Civil Service the "set the people free" policy was still in operation, and accorded with my reforming zeal. I felt I could help reduce the field of governmental activity.' There was plenty of evidence to suggest that civil servants are keenly interested in political issues – though they would no more comment in this frank way in public than let it be publicly known how they individually voted.

Secondly, statements made by the 1956 entrants shed a flood of light on an issue which astute commentators have been grappling with for a long time. One Minister, talking to Anthony Sampson about his civil servants, said: 'You know, they've got a wonderful political sense, without themselves being political.'[11] Another said: 'They're extraordinarily adaptable. I remember when we took office in 1951, the same civil servant who had been looking after nationalisation had already got out a plan for de-nationalisation. He went about it with just the same enthusiasm.'[12]

C. P. Snow has referred to their world of politics as 'closed politics' ('the politics of the civil servants, the scientists, the industrialists').[13] All these remarks have an element of truth. One ex-temporary civil servant (Assistant Director in the Department of Economic Affairs, 1964–66) explained to the Fulton Committee the 'closed politics' phenomenon as he saw it:

'There is also, as in any organisation, a purely Civil Service politics, division versus division, department versus department, individuals versus their colleagues, etc. What is interesting is the way these political struggles are rarely brought into the open, and never admitted, unlike for example academic politics, which is over-rationalised and over-publicised by the participants . . . The game is played with the utmost suavity and friendliness, open bad temper and annoyance being extremely rare and socially frowned upon. Partly this is due to the highly mature and sensitive recognition of the common responsibilities of the Service and the fact that an "enemy" of today from a department across the table may be tomorrow's colleague in the same department.'[14]

One further aspect of the politics of civil servants concerns their sensitivity to possible changes in government and the policy changes that might be involved – a phenomenon which is not to be found in most comparable 'western' countries. When the end of a Government's period in office is in sight and the journalists are crystal-gazing for the date of the next election, senior civil servants begin making their own confidential preparations within the corridors of power. Senior civil servants intensify their study of Opposition policy and make contingency plans in case there is a new party in power after the election. It is an urbane and practical Whitehall practice that has no equivalent in, for example, Washington, where administrators are likely to be changed by a new President (indeed, after the 1964 general election one or two very senior American civil servants came to London to do some research into it). Towards the end of 1969 it was reported[15] that politically sharp members of the Athenaeum Club and the Reform Club might see this process in operation if they surveyed their dining rooms; they might well see an eminent civil servant entertaining for luncheon or dinner a Tory adviser, or back-room man, if not a front-bench M.P. Mr Iain Macleod's commitment to a value-added tax and his belief that it could begin to operate a year after the Budget in which it might be introduced, can be no more than a pipe-dream if the Treasury and Inland Revenue have not previously made advance studies of it. However, such activities, important as they are for any future Government and in the best interests of the country, can only take place in a situation where the political role of civil servants is not misunderstood.

Thirdly, the survey of 1956 entrants suggested that the political attitudes of higher civil servants in Britain are positive, but distinctive to them as a group. Because these civil servants work so closely with Ministers they regard all politicians as members of one profession (the Government of today might be the Opposition tomorrow)

I

irrespective of party or ideology. The research suggested a hitherto unexplored phenomenon, not only are these political attitudes different from non-officials, they are also different from the political attitudes of officials in most other countries: for example, they would be alien to most developing countries and also alien to those modern western countries which operate to any extent on the spoils system. Civil servants take part in the 'closed politics' of their work, but their attitudes to party politics are special, and peculiar to them.

C. K. Munro dealt with his experience of this phenomenon in *The Fountains of Trafalgar Square*. He recalled:

'I learnt that peculiar neutrality as regards political issues which is the hall-mark of a Service which has to serve all parties alike. I learnt that the whole nation might be rent with political controversy and the papers full of scare-heads blaring forth Party slogans, yet, when one entered one's Ministry, one found the whole business hardly mentioned; that civil servants are so much concerned with the practical problems involved in implementing the policy of *any* Party that, if they discuss politics at all, it tends to be in terms of the practical and unpractical, a subject about which cool argument is possible, rather than of right and wrong, which only leads to heat and denunciation between those who differ with regard to them. As a consequence, I learnt that one can work day in day out with a number of colleagues without ever discovering on what side they are in politics, or if they are on any side at all. All these things I learnt, not because anyone told me, but because they impregnated the official atmosphere in which I lived.'[16]

However favourable to one party a civil servant is in his early years, because he works so closely with politicians, he soon becomes aware of the ineptitude of any party. After a time, it seems, he learns to think more in terms of policies and their workability, he focuses his political interests on the merits and demerits of particular policies, and since all political parties tend to have a mixture of policies, the parties as such are seen in a distinctly neutral light.

SOCIAL BACKGROUND AND CLASS

It may be important to know about the social background and class of higher civil servants because however impartial they may seek to be in giving advice about policies, they may nevertheless harbour a certain amount of unconscious bias. No serious suggestion is made that this is a dangerous defect in the Civil Service at the present time for no one really knows enough about it, but that it is a potentially important factor has been recognised for a considerable period of time (and is reflected, for example, in the interesting evidence about social and educational background taken by the MacDonnell Royal Commission: it was also an important theme in Laski's introductory essay to J. P. Mallalieu's *Passed to You, Please*[17] and in R. K. Kelsall's study *Higher Civil Servants in Britain*).[18] We need to know whether officials in important positions who make decisions affecting the lives of everyone in the country are a representative section of the whole population or representative only of a part (or have they been peculiarly neutralised in some process of socialisation that would have been approved by Plato?); we need also to know how such officials fit into the general spectrum of the class structure in our society.

One element in social background concerns the families from which higher civil servants come, and their own educational background. Both these factors were considered during the research for 'Profile of a Profession'. They were also considered by the 1965 Select Committee on Estimates, and by the Fulton Committee.

The Social Survey of the Civil Service conducted by A. H. Halsey and I. M. Crewe drew attention to the substantial proportion of the Administrative Class who are drawn from 'Civil Service' families: 22 per cent are the sons or daughters of civil servants, the great majority of whom were also in the Administrative Class or other classes of similar social status – thus the Administrative Class has the highest degree of 'self recruitment' among all Civil Service Classes covered in the Social Survey.[19] Women, who form 8 per cent of the Administrative Class, are concentrated in the lower grades where they comprise 10 per cent of the staff, and they tend to have social origins which are 'superior' to those of their male counterparts (this pattern is found also in other Civil Service Classes, and in the United States Federal

Services, and seems to reflect a greater degree of selection in women's education).[20]

Of the 1956 entrants who answered the questionnaire, twenty-seven out of thirty-five were first generation university students in their immediate family. And an analysis of the fathers' occupation at the time of their entry into the Civil Service shows that, in terms of the Registrar General's Socio-Economic Classification, 7 were in Class I, 19 in Class II, 6 in Class III, 1 in Class IV and 2 in Class V.

All thirty-five came from different schools which were difficult to classify beyond saying that 12 are independent (public) schools, 10 are direct grant schools and 13 are local authority (grammar) schools. But these statistics suggest that 1956 may have been a slightly untypical year for recruitment to the Administrative Class, when compared with other years about that time. Evidence presented to the 1965 Select Committee on Estimates shows that the proportion of direct entrant Assistant Principals who attended L.E.A. maintained and aided schools went down from 42 per cent in the period 1948–56 to 30 per cent in the period 1957–63. The 1965 sample is also very different from the sample of eighty higher civil servants studied by Dale in the 1930s. (Of Dale's higher civil servants twenty were educated at one or other of the large English boarding schools; Eton produced six, Winchester three, Rugby, Marlborough and Clifton two each, and no other more than one. Eighteen were educated at one or other of the large English day schools – the main contributions were four from Merchant Taylors', and three each from St Pauls', Dulwich and King Edward's School, Birmingham. Twelve came from Scottish and Irish schools – George Watson's College in Edinburgh contributing two and no other school more than one. The remaining thirty came from a great variety of schools (one Australian), most of which were day-schools. Two of these thirty were at county schools.)[21]

Tables XIII and XIV give details for various years showing fathers' occupation and schools attended by direct entrants to the Administrative Class.

The Fulton Committee was also supplied with information about the school education of Permanent, Deputy and Under Secretaries. The information is reproduced in Table XV.

Although the 1956 entrants were all willing to talk about their own political attitudes and political attitudes generally in the Administrative Class, they were much less willing to talk about social class, and some

TABLE XIII[22]

SCHOOLS

	Method I				Method II			
	Competitors		Successful		Competitors		Successful	
	1948–56*	1957–63	1948–56*	1957–63	1948–56*	1957–63	1948–56*	1957–63
British								
Boarding	261	247	74	53	693	905	91	120
Day:								
(*a*) Independent and direct grant	470	308	86	54	737	838	54	91
(*b*) L.E.A. maintained or aided	980	375	157	60	1,298	877	62	80
Foreign	9	11	2	2	18	29	1	3
Totals	1,720	941	319	169	2,746	2,649	208	294

* As Appendix IV, Table II of Cmnd. 232.

TABLE XIV[23]

FATHER'S OCCUPATION

Occupational Group*	Method I								Method II							
	Competitors				Successes				Competitors				Successes			
	1948–56		1957–63		1948–56		1957–63		1948–56		1957–63		1948–56		1957–63	
I	434		338		103		60		918		1,042		99		152	
II	754		355		131		72		1,169		1,011		74		104	
III	479		181		76		25		590		487		29		30	
IV	34		40		5		7		40		63		1		6	
V	13		4		4		—		16		9		3		2	
Unknown	6		23		—		5		13		37		2		—	
Totals	1,720		941		319		169		2,746		2,649		208		294	

* As defined by Registrar General:
  I. Administrators, managers, senior professional and scientific occupations.
  II. Intermediate professional, managerial and technical occupations.
  III. Highly skilled workers, foremen, supervisors, clerks.
  IV. Skilled and semi-skilled.
  V. Unskilled.

TABLE XV[24]

SCHOOL EDUCATION OF PERMANENT, DEPUTY AND UNDER SECRETARIES—FIGURES PROVIDED BY THE TREASURY

a. Schools attended by Permanent, Deputy and Under Secretaries in the Home Civil Service (January, 1966)

	Permanent Secretaries	Deputy Secretaries	Under Secretaries	Total
	%	%	%	%
British				
Boarding	13 (40)	20 (30)	82 (32)	115 (32)
Day				
(*a*) Independent and direct grant	8 (24)	16 (24)	54 (21)	78 (22)
(*b*) L.E.A. maintained or aided	11 (33)	29 (44)	112 (43)	152 (43)
Overseas	1 (3)	1 (2)	2 (1)	4 (1)
Not known	—	—	7 (3)	7 (2)
	33 (100)	66 (100)	257 (100)	356 (100)

b. Comparing these figures with those for new recruits given by the Civil Service Commission to the Estimates Committee (pages 27 and 31 of the Bray Report), the percentages are:

	Higher Civil Service 1966	Recruits to Administrative Class 1948–63
	%	%
British		
Boarding	32	34
Day		
(*a*) Independent and direct grant	22	29
(*b*) L.E.A. maintained or aided	43	36
Overseas	1	1
Not known	2	—
	100	100

The differences are much what one would expect having regard to the fact that the first column includes people who entered the Administrative Class by promotion from other classes.

preferred not to talk about it at all. The civil servants were asked which social class they would say they belonged to and which social class they would say people in the Administrative Civil Service generally belonged to. The answers were:

Which social class would you say you belong to?

Upper middle or professional middle	12
Middle or middle-middle	16
Lower middle	1
None	5
Prefer not to answer	1

Which social class would you say people in the Administrative Civil Service generally belong to?

Upper middle or professional middle	14
Middle or middle-middle	18
Lower middle	0
None	2
Prefer not to answer	1

In discussion, they were also asked what criteria they had borne in mind in reaching their answers. A large number of different criteria were given among which education, income, family background and the subjective assessment of society in general were the most common (for example one reply was 'I belong to the class of people who are (i) educated at state school and non-Oxbridge university and (ii) earn approximately £3,000 p.a. in non-manual work of an executive kind'). Equally common were answers such as 'I don't think in terms of social class', or 'I should try to avoid saying anything, but under pressure I would say . . .', or 'I would say I belong to no social class because I think consciousness of class is the curse of this country'.

Three particularly interesting answers were given to the question about the Administrative Civil Service generally. They were: 'They are all probably middle *now*, with family backgrounds differing widely'; 'If you exclude top civil servants from the upper class, the upper class is drained of any meaning at all; the upper class must include the "establishment" and top civil servants are part of the establishment'; 'My father once asked me if the people I worked with were gentlemen. I had to admit they weren't, mostly. There is a curious tendency for the women to be of somewhat higher social class than the men.'

One of the most interesting and unexpected aspects of the research for 'Profile of a Profession' was the difficulty of obtaining answers to the questions on social class. In one sense Administrative civil servants can be regarded as a classless group within society. Some of the civil servants who had been perfectly willing to answer all sorts of questions about their private lives and political attitudes became distinctly uncomfortable when talking about social class, and a few simply said they preferred not to discuss it (this was the only aspect of the research on which anyone said he would rather not pursue the subject). Naturally, whilst trying not to cause offence, the researcher tactfully tried to find out why there was this feeling. The most likely conclusion seems to be that a number of these civil servants have family backgrounds which they feel are below the social class to which they feel they now belong. On the other hand, at work they often deal with people of a higher social class than themselves. They may work in Whitehall, in rooms decorated with reminders of the historic past, and in the evening return home to a pleasant but rather small suburban semi. Consequently many of them feel unattached to any particular social class and are quite happy to be in that position, for it means they can easily adjust themselves to various classes and this is both pleasant and sometimes an advantage in their work. Only two seemed really disturbed by this, but about a third of the sample tried to avoid the question or said they just didn't think in terms of class.

One extremely interesting observation connected with social background was made by Dale and is worth recalling, not because we now have evidence to prove or disprove it but because the points he noted in making his observation now appear to be more extreme. It is a plausible line for investigation, and if valid may be of outstanding importance in many respects.

Dale noted[25] that the kind of young man who entered the Civil Service was almost certain to possess ability and industry above the average of his contemporaries at school and university; 'any success implies at the lowest a long and elaborate education and the capacity for hard work when required'. Secondly, many of the entrants are poor and without family influence, so that a young man of this origin must earn his own living from the moment he leaves university:

sometimes his family are looking for help from him as soon as he has finished his education. To such a young man careers in journalism and literature may appear too insecure, business pays too little at the beginning, there are few vacancies for academic posts (where, in any case, Dale noted that influence was not excluded from their distribution), school teaching in a public school may seem distasteful except to the few men who have a natural liking for boys (and for athletics) and have themselves been educated at a public school. There remains only the Civil Service. Many candidates, he concluded, desire the security of the Civil Service not because they are unadventurous but because they are 'poor'. Such candidates have been aware from their school-days of strong motives to concentrated industry, and they cannot indulge other tastes even in the holidays to more than a subordinate degree.

In consequence, entrants according to Dale tended to have two defects. One is lack of self confidence, arising from the lack of a 'background' in early years. The second is a certain lack of animal spirits, and of mental and nervous energy – the kind of energy which allows a man to spend hours in the close discussion of difficult affairs and yet at the end be fresh, alert, with all his wits about him. 'This deficiency may not become evident for fifteen or twenty years after he has entered the Service . . . after the age of forty the results of the strain put on him in boyhood and youth become apparent, at the same time as his responsibilities grow. He will do his work quite well, within limits . . . [but] unless he is very fortunate he will not rise to the highest places in the Civil Service, any more than he would in other professions. He will stick at the rank of Assistant Secretary or thereabouts; or, if he is personally agreeable, he may end his career in dignified obscurity at the head of one of the minor offices which revolve as satellites around the great Departments, notably around the Treasury.'[26]

In Dale's book this seems an interesting and fair observation. If it is a correct assessment the situation may now apply more generally and be potentially alarming. There can be little doubt that the office hours of higher civil servants are now considerably in excess of those worked in the 1930s, and in addition the majority of higher civil servants must spend an appreciable amount of time in travel to and from the office. By the time they reach the middle and higher ranks they may be even more tired than their predecessors of whom Dale was writing (and because of the expansion of governmental activity they may perhaps hold even more responsible positions).

Without being aware of Dale's analysis a significant number of civil servants made comments during the survey for 'Profile of a Profession' which could well support his conclusions. For example, one official commenting on leisure-time activities said: 'most higher civil servants tend to lead rather dull private lives because they don't have the time or energy to do interesting things' and another commented that social contacts of civil servants are now considerably less than they were pre-war. Two others, explaining features of the Civil Service which they disliked, gave 'the expectation that civil servants will work inordinate hours without regard to their family life' and 'the rapidity with which middle age seems to ossify so many colleagues once promoted to Principal'. The same point was made by Lord Salter when he wrote, in his memoirs in 1961, of the 'Civil Service . . . destroying or stultifying a large proportion of what it recruited. The deadening effect of a mass of routine work, almost unchanging from year to year, of a cumbrous system of red-tape and a vast, and usually unimaginative, hierarchy of superior authority, destroyed by middle life, for the majority of civil servants, half of their potential capacity for initiative.'[27]

7. Conclusion

'Now the main difference between a State which has
to do things and a State which has to prevent things
being done arises from the fact that the prevention of
wrongdoing can be carried out by one man with
disciplined human instruments merely carrying out
his orders. A negative Government only requires
courage and consistency in its officials; but a positive
Government requires a constant supply of invention
and suggestions, and invention and suggestion take
time.'[1]

THE PHILOSOPHY OF THE HIGHER CIVIL SERVICE

The first chapter of the Fulton Report strongly criticised what
it called 'the tradition of the "all-rounder"' and 'the cult of the amateur'. It was the manner in which this criticism was expressed which
led some commentators to regard the Report as a political tract or
contemporary essay. This was unfortunate, for in using such popular
terms the Report, unintentionally, gave support to the superficial
criticism of institutions then in vogue, and catch-phrases from the
Report were taken up by the popular press often without adequate
attention being focused on the essence of the problem.

The fact is that to the outsider the British Civil Service appears
a curious institution, endued with an optimistic attitude that an
untrained man with talent, who is uprooted at work every eighteen
months or so, should be able to deal with any situation. It uses its
manpower badly, sometimes in squalid overcrowded accommodation,
but the good quality of the manpower itself makes it possible for the
Service to work reasonably effectively. However, the fact that it does
may be more a tribute to the Civil Service Commission's selection
procedures and the education its candidates get at the universities,
than the way the Service has been managed.

Popular conceptions and the first chapter of the Fulton Report
tend to support the music-hall-joke image of the Service and give a

quite unfounded impression of complacency within it. Some critics of the Administrative Class have also fostered such views by emphasising, for example, that 'its advice is based on amateur hunch rather than professional assessment and research'.[2] Such critics have usually failed to analyse the problem of 'amateurism', and misunderstand the underlying virtues and significance of the administrative system as it at present operates in Britain.

There are several facets of this problem which should receive more serious attention. Perhaps the most important is the issue of deciding the necessary qualities needed for a senior official in the public service. Given that no adequate research has been done on this question in relation to either central or local government in Britain, the Civil Service has worked out its own pragmatic method for dealing with the problem.

The basic philosophy or theory of administration at the higher levels arises from the experience of the Indian Civil Service in the nineteenth century. In India the tasks for which the civil servants were responsible were almost infinitely various, so no specialist pre-entry qualifications were looked for. Macaulay's initiative led to a formalisation of entry requirements and general academic ability became the basic quality sought; and specialist (as applied to the Indian environment) knowledge and skills were to be learned during a post-entry period of probation.

Similarly, for Administrative positions in the Home Civil Service, the requirements are academic ability in any subject plus certain other general qualities. The scope and tasks to be performed in the Administrative Civil Service are also very varied but there is now a considerable amount of post-entry socialisation and training (concentrating on a study of the environment in which the work is to be carried out: mainly economics, with a certain amount of social and economic administration).

Nearly everyone involved in, or with a general academic interest in, the work of the higher Civil Service turns his mind from time to time to the essential quality needed for it. But no specific or peculiar quality has yet been discovered.

The 1956 entrants into the Administrative Class were asked during the survey for 'Profile of a Profession' for their views on this. One catalogued the necessary virtues as he saw them: 'Analytical ability, judgment, initiative, discretion, persuasiveness, intelligence, ability to get on with people, sense of humour, ability to write and speak clearly (God, move over).' Another said: 'An Administrator should have his feet on the ground so that his advice, for example, to a Minister, is not only well worked out logically but makes sense in terms of public wishes (or at least recognises them and goes as far as it can to meet them) and in terms of political difficulties and the reactions of pressure groups. An Administrator must be willing to work on a number of things at once and to turn from one topic to another on demand. He has to recognise the many deadlines which must be met regardless of other commitments, official and personal.' Some talked of administrators they admired (several had been impressed by reading Roy Harrod's biography of Keynes) but several said the nearest they could get to expressing it was that a person needed a 'flair' for administration. One added that bad civil servants failed because of lack of judgment, and judgment cannot be taught.

We should not, however, in a desire for some measurable quality, neglect the possibility that the pragmatic approach, together with the experience and work of the Civil Service Commission, has already led to the best approach possible at the present time. Psychologists researching into what makes a good leader have tended to come to the conclusion that the key lies in the situation and that a leadership role is bestowed on a person rather than is to be found primarily through some peculiar quality in the make-up of a character. So with administration, it may be that the administrator's 'flair' is to be found primarily through the administrative situation and other people with whom he deals, rather than with some measurable characteristic in his own make-up.

In the Civil Service the Administrator is likely to find himself in a distinctively managerial situation at a considerably earlier age than his contemporaries in industry. As Sir Lawrence Helsby told the Estimates Committee in 1965, the skill of the Administrative civil servant, even in his thirties, is of an eclectic and wide-ranging kind which in industry and commerce is rarely found below board level.[3]

His peculiar contribution to the work of the vast institution known as the Civil Service is a combination of certain innate abilities plus experience in the Service and a specialised knowledge of the political and social environment in which his own work and that of his department proceeds. This is a field of knowledge which scientists and professionals in the Civil Service can never explore to the same extent because they do not have the time while they are practising their specialist skills (though this does not mean that given the opportunity and inclination they would be incapable of performing adequately the administrative role). Indeed, it has been convincingly argued that far from being 'amateur' in approach, the so-called generalist is himself highly skilled in a professional way. Lord Bridges, for example, once spoke of '. . . the special techniques of the skilled administrator – perhaps it should be called an art – the man or woman who may indeed possess special knowledge in several fields, but who will be a good adviser in any field because he or she knows how and where to find reliable knowledge, can assess the expertise of others at its true worth, can spot the strong and weak points in any situation at short notice, and can advise how to handle a complex situation'.[4]

Thus one of the primary qualities required in a higher civil servant is an appreciation of the constraints within which the work of central government administration must be carried on. It is not merely a recognition of the existence of the constraints – which may in part be similar to those experienced in, for example, local government admini-stration or business management – but an awareness of how the constraints affect the system in practice and how they can be manipu-lated to achieve the desired ends of the central government itself. Consequently, an able higher civil servant will either consciously or unconsciously have briefed himself on the nature of the constraints in his area of administration and know how they work. In Britain central government has to achieve its objectives much more through encouragement and persuasion than the central governments of most other countries (the central government tends to have a less dominant role in more capitalist countries and a more dominant role in more socialist countries; in both cases the qualities needed in senior officials are likely to be different from the qualities needed in Britain).

Marshall E. Dimock has written[5] of the importance of the ethical content of administrative methods, and praised the way in which moral philosophy has been emphasised in the British Civil Service (he places, for example, Lords Haldane, Salter and Franks in this tradition). According to him this has more to do with Britain's institutional durability than many of the things that are more emphasised in America such as the British Career Civil Service or the ruling aristo-cracy. He noted with pleasure that the Harvard Business School had established a course on administrative ethics conducted by a professor in the Harvard Divinity School. A number of people have come to conclusions about the British Civil Service similar to those of Dimock – the influence of the nineteenth-century Oxford idealists when the foundations of our Civil Service system were being laid, and the significant proportions of Oxbridge arts graduates in the higher Civil Service in the twentieth century may be of more consequence than is popularly realised.

One of the questions which must be considered by those planning training courses for higher civil servants is what form of training in terms of both subject matter and educational process is most suitable as an aid to professional development. Perhaps the present emphasis on economics, interesting though it may be, is not the most appropriate specialism. One may wonder whether specialists in economics have shown themselves to be conspicuously more outstanding as administrators than the classicists who previously seemed to some influential commentators to be peculiarly well qualified for senior administrative positions. The most fashionable subject at any given time may have an important influence on our society, if only because, as Macaulay argued, 'The youth who does best what all the ablest and most ambitious youths about him are trying to do well will generally prove a superior man.' But perhaps the time is now opportune for the professional element in higher Civil Service work to be made the subject of serious study. Perhaps the training emphasis on traditional teaching methods should be re-examined alongside other teaching methods such as simulation exercises, management games and the use of case studies in various ways. We may need to consider the consequences for society, as well as for the administrative system, of the particular specialisms and the degree of specialisation we now have.

When there is increasing specialisation in every walk of life and at all levels, and officials are tending to act bureaucratically, then the man at the top of an organization in the public service often has a special responsibility for ensuring that the rules are applied with an element of temperance and humanity as well as with equity. And there is evidence to suggest that organizations which have placed a premium on the specialist approach, where senior officials attempt to make decisions scientifically by emphasising the importance of professional assessment and research and the principles of scientific management, have had to reconsider their position. The Canadian Civil Service, for example, seems recently to have been reassessing the position of the generalist. One leading commentator in that country has been J. J. Deutsch, who held a number of posts in the Canadian Civil Service, his last one as Secretary of the Treasury Board. He is now Chairman of the Economic Council of Canada and Principal of Queen's University. In an address about ten years ago he said:

'I have gained the impression that the Canadian service is particularly strong in the professional and expert categories and in the field of policy-making where the contribution of such personnel is specially valuable. I believe that in these respects the Canadian service is unmatched anywhere else. It seems to me, however, that the service is not equally strong in the field of general administration. I do not wish to belittle the importance of having an adequate number of experts and highly qualified professionals. Obviously, this is essential for the complex tasks which modern governments are required to perform. I am merely pleading that more attention should be paid to the development of general administrators. Because of weaknesses in this respect the service has been using a considerable number of experts and professionals for administrative tasks . . . Experts and professionals are by definition specialists in particular fields, and it is in these fields that they can generally make their most valuable contribution.'[6]

In Canada attempts are being made to adjust to the situation in which they have found themselves. There are now opportunities in universities to take broad-based degrees in the sciences which provide a good background for a study of administration or management and ultimately for careers leading to senior positions in administration.

However, it must not be thought that the phrases used in the first chapter of the Fulton Report imply that all Administrators in the British Civil Service are dealing with specialist matters with which they have no technical familiarity. This is no more true than the often expressed view that the majority of Administrators have classics degrees. Lord Bridges has told us that in 1964, in the two branches of the Treasury dealing with economic co-ordination, ten out of twelve of the staff had professional economic training. Bridges also said that if you took the four top grades in the Administrative Class at that time (Assistant Secretary to Permanent Secretary), 13 per cent had degrees in science or mathematics.[7]

On the other hand there are elements of weak management in the

K

higher Civil Service which have been justly criticised in the past and which it is hoped are now being reformed. Two examples are the placement and posting of staff, and training.

After criticising what he regarded as amateurism in the Civil Service, a 1956 entrant who took part in the survey for 'Profile of a Profession' and who had been given seven jobs in one ministry, 'none lasting longer than two years, and none bearing any but the most remote relation to any others', added: 'with this kind of career there is not enough scope for getting to know a job thoroughly and for acquiring enough confidence (and time) to produce new ideas and "make a difference". Nor is this expected – the main skill of most administrators is to keep things moving, not to give them new impetus in a new direction.' It is hardly surprising that the theory of posting civil servants with such regularity and without careful career planning creates resentment and allegations of amateurism even within the Service.

In the Administrative Class the average man's career is shaped by such abilities as he has which happen to coincide with chance or random opportunities which happen to present themselves to him. Much other ability either remains latent or may be soured through a cynicism which grows with experience of how the Civil Service uses its personnel. A minority of higher civil servants are under-employed whilst a majority work inordinately long hours. In some cases their talents are wasted through bad management of work and unnecessary time spent in tedious routine clerical duties.

Training is another difficult problem which in the higher Civil Service has improved beyond all recognition in the last few years. Without changing the basic principles on which the Service operates, a great deal can (and now is) being done to step up through training courses the higher civil servant's awareness of various aspects of the environment in which he works. This is what the officials concerned have been demanding. The Treasury started moving in that direction in the mid-1960s and its efforts (accelerated by the new Civil Service Department) were consecrated by the Fulton Committee.

All such developments may be generally applauded though in fact they are no more than long overdue moves in the direction in which the Service was already moving. But if there is to be any fundamental change it should be preceded by serious rethinking of the management objectives in the higher Civil Service, in particular there must be a rethinking of the 'end' of public administration and of the role of the Civil Service in the British constitution.

THE HIGHER CIVIL SERVICE IN THE CONSTITUTION

The qualities to be looked for in recruiting for the Administrative Civil Service depend primarily on what the Administrative Civil Service does or is expected to do. If its most important work is to help effect compromises between group pressures in the political arena, to give critical advice to the Government, and be able to perform a large and varied number of management tasks of which no one has a reliable and accurate record, then the qualities needed are probably those sought at present during the recruitment procedures. Furthermore, when the tasks to be performed are as varied as they are at present, and when highly qualified young university graduates offer themselves in as large numbers as they do at present, it might require some ingenuity to select people whom their selectors subsequently regard as inadequate.

If, however, the most important work of the Administrative Class is the minimal one of the mid-nineteenth-century negative state, then perhaps the qualities need not be so many nor need they be necessarily present to such an advanced stage of development. But if, on the other hand, the Administrative Civil Service is to seek out new knowledge about society, to initiate bold new policies that affect fundamentally the lives of every citizen in the country, to manage the administrative machinery of the state beyond the point where anyone can grasp what it is all about at any one time, then the Civil Service may need seriously to consider whether it needs people with entirely different backgrounds in temperament and training, and be even more certain that it is selecting the best people to perform those functions.

Students of the British constitution, who are concerned with an examination of the structure and functions of the organs of central and local government, are likely to agree that the machinery of the state and its manner of working in this country constitute a finely balanced system. In some senses it resembles the human body: make an error of judgment, inflict an injury, inject a foreign body, and correcting action will be taken. So with the British system of government and the sub-system of the Civil Service: policies it deems irrelevant or dangerous are dealt with in one way or another, and adjustments are made to accommodate 'foreign bodies' such as the Parliamentary Commissioner or a specialist Select Committee. In the British constitution the Civil Service has a number of functions which ensure its position in the balance of power, and extreme changes within it could have serious and unintended effects on the constitution.

At all levels, but particularly towards the top, it is necessary to remember constantly that work in public administration is not the same as work in business management, and although some techniques or processes may be transferable, they are all likely to be affected at any time by the constraints imposed by the political environment in which the work has to be performed.

This happens, for example, at the highest levels of decision-making in the Civil Service. There is a sense in which the classical terminology used by political scientists is now somewhat irrelevant. A country like Britain can no longer, except in fantasy, regard itself as a self-contained island, whether it be set in a silver sea in the Shakespearian sense, or whether it be an off-shore island in the twentieth-century European sense. Insufficient appreciation is often given to the way Ministers and civil servants alike are in their decision-making activities more closely circumscribed by the facts of the case than the general public usually realise. They are also considerably affected by external pressures, including very often the attitudes of the governments of other countries over which they have no control.[8]

These constraints may be seen in the daily lives of civil servants in their offices. The Fulton Committee, for example, was told that 'at the moment a whole generation of Principals, aged between 28 and 40, is messing about writing first drafts of speeches and amassing technical briefs for Ministers'.[9] A civil servant taking part in the survey for 'Profile of a Profession' explained that 'Much of the average Principal's time seems fruitless in that Parliamentary Questions, MPs' queries, etc., take up an inordinate amount of time which could be spent on more constructive policy thinking – but that is unavoidable, as the price of our democratic system'. The environment exercises its constraints at all levels in the hierarchy and can be seen nowhere better than in the day-to-day routine matters dealt with by the official bureaucracy. One Principal has recently explained: 'one can take few decisions without consultation. One presents the relevant details – mainly gathered from the back files – of the topic in question, to one's Assistant Secretary, who pits his judgment against the Under Secretary and so on up the tree'.[10] And throughout the Service there is the constant thought influencing all aspects of official behaviour that some action or decision, even of a minor order, could lead to a Parliamentary Question or attract the attentions of the Parliamentary Commissioner or the Comptroller and Auditor General (to say nothing of the myriads of tribunals, committees and unofficial bodies), and consequently all actions and most thoughts need recording – if only as a safeguard for the future.

The nature of the constitutional constraints on Civil Service work is well illustrated by the problem of developing accountable management in the Service. Accountable management means holding individuals and units responsible for performance measured as objectively as possible.[11] Since the Fulton Report made proposals on this concept work has been proceeding in departments to examine how this might be applied in practice, and there is now an inter-departmental committee[12] which has agreed on a programme of work which the Civil Service Department is undertaking. However, there are difficulties about implementing accountable management in the Civil Service which are not experienced in other fields of management activity. As the Fulton Committee recognised, decisions often have to be referred to a higher level than their intrinsic difficulty or apparent importance merits because they involve the responsibility of Ministers to Parliament, and Parliamentary accountability fosters centralised controls by Accounting Officers. Again, many problems facing the public service can be solved only after consultation between departments, with other public bodies, and with various outside interests, so that there is a considerable amount of joint decision-making.

Constraints are also experienced in periodic 'economy drives'. For example, when the Civil Service imported temporarily some help from the universities and industry during the 1960s, it also started discussions to second some younger administrators to industry for short periods. Though this was hailed as a worthy recommendation when made by the Fulton Committee, the committee was, in fact, formalising in its Report something that had been already attempted by the Treasury. The trouble was that after October 1964 (when the Labour Government came to power with its mass of plans for reforms), as Sir William Armstrong told the Estimates Committee in 1965, 'We simply could not let the people go.'[13] Another example has been the painful way the Civil Service has given birth to training programmes;

training has always been near the top of the list when economies are considered so that the Association of First Division Civil Servants has justifiably christened it 'a Cinderella among Civil Service activities'.

When operating within these constraints imposed by the political environment in which its work is performed, it is not surprising that the Civil Service has evolved various antidotes which may be seen in certain aspects of its work; the environment permeates the official behaviour of civil servants in their everyday lives. Two examples of this are the political attitudes of higher civil servants and their tendency to secrecy and anonymity.

As far as the political attitudes are concerned, the Masterman Report seems to have appreciated the situation when it said that hardly any potential civil servants 'are deterred from entering the Service by the restrictions now imposed. Nor do we think that those few who are deterred would necessarily make the best civil servants'.[14] On the contrary, civil servants seem to have perfected a process of socialisation which neutralises them as far as party politics is concerned, and an appropriate professional ethic is instilled in the new entrant from early in his career. As far as secrecy and anonymity is concerned there appears to be some rethinking inside the Service on this subject. It has already been said that the Indian Civil Service was a silent and anonymous service and in it may be seen the beginnings of the often caricatured Civil Service anonymity. In addition, the doctrine of Ministerial responsibility as it has been developed during the past hundred years has ensured that it is nearly always politicians who explain government policies to the public. The traditional anonymity has, however, been the subject of considerable criticism in recent years. A Fabian Group[15] was very critical of official secrecy, so was the Fulton Report,[16] though it welcomed the trend of recent years towards wider and more open consultation in the Government's administrative processes. Much more could, however, and now is, being done in this direction, as has been explained in the White Paper 'Information and the Public Interest'[17] (further discussed later in this chapter).

One danger that must be guarded against when discussing constraints on the public service is the temptation to magnify the difficulties and denigrate the efforts being made within the Service to improve its standards. The music-hall-joke image of the Service seems to have been given such publicity that when the Civil Service does take a lead in some aspect of management, credit is rarely given. But, according to the Treasury, when 26 temporary civil servants (the majority of whom were from commerce and industry) were recently brought together to discuss their impressions, they agreed in rejecting the view that the government service could be radically improved by simply adopting 'business-like' methods: they accepted on the contrary that the style of Civil Service work was bound to be affected by the constraints of parliamentary accountability, and the pursuit of objectivity rather than profit. Even more gratifying, they considered the Civil Service to be more modern in its techniques, where these were relevant, than the outside world realised. Again, aspects of the Civil Service such as the administrative hierarchy were less rigid, and made more sense, than they had previously supposed.

There is, then, a style of management to be seen in the higher levels of public administration which is in many respects different from business management even where the techniques being used are fundamentally similar. The relationship between the various subsystems of the political system (legislature, judiciary, executive) must be considered in the context of the system as a whole, and is reflected in the style of management. This style is in turn established and perpetuated through the combination of a number of factors not the least of which is the process of socialisation provided by the Service itself. The style may also be important for maintaining certain aspects of the balance of power, within the British system of government. When Sir William Armstrong, the present Head of the Civil Service, was recently questioned on television about his personal attitude to exercising the considerable power he has, he explained that for him being accountable to oneself is the greatest taskmaster. He added: 'I am accountable to my own ideal of a civil servant.'[18]

AFTER THE FULTON REPORT

Royal Commissions or their equivalents are used as agents of government for various reasons. Sometimes the appointment of such a body enables a problem to be taken out of the limelight, perhaps the Government hopes an issue will be forgotten or that an independent body will produce a face-saving formula helpful to all concerned; or it is hoped the Commission will invent useful policies that for one reason or another the politicians are not able to produce. Sometimes its appointment is an aid to removing obstacles or in providing a necessary type of support for an issue that politicians or administrators wish to further but feel they cannot easily push ahead without such support.

Once appointed, the Commission may go about its work in a number of ways, though the characteristic procedures are well known and have been outlined in a stimulating way by Andrew Shonfield. He has described how their behaviour tends to be modelled on the image of a jury hearing the views of the whole nation and this is bound to take a good deal of time; everyone with views must be given the opportunity to present them:

'The pace is leisurely, because it is essential to avoid an impression of hurrying anyone, and the subject matter with which the commission concerns itself over a considerable part of its life is largely determined by the interests of the witnesses presenting their views. The whole thing is treated very much as a part-time activity: it has to be, in any case, since it is unpaid. Moreover, the members start by being so concerned with the achievement of consensus on the issues on which they have to report that they tend to delay the process of intellectual confrontation. There is a feeling that if one goes on hearing witnesses long enough, some of the most contentious issues may disappear or at any rate the points of contention be so greatly reduced that there is little left to argue about. The judicial model dominates the procedure: you keep filling your mind with facts and views supplied by witnesses, and must be careful to avoid any attempt to identify provisional points of agreement and disagreement among the judges. The aim is, after all, to arrive at a set of practical recommendations which all can sign, without offending any member's principles. Too much analysis early on might jeopardise the whole exercise.'[19]

The appointment of the Fulton Committee was not unexpected. There is now almost a convention for a major inquiry once in every generation of civil servants: the Priestley Royal Commission in 1955 was only a partial inquiry; the previous wide-ranging review was that of the Tomlin Commission in 1931. The Fabian pamphlet *The Administrators*, critical of the Civil Service, was published in 1964; in the same year Harold Wilson was interviewed for the BBC by Norman Hunt and outlined his plans for the modernisation of Britain if he won the 1964 General Election;[20] and a sub-committee of the Select Committee on Estimates, which considered recruitment to the Civil Service, reported in 1965.

That the Fulton Committee conformed so closely to the traditional method of working of Royal Commissions was, however, rather unexpected. It was considering problems of the Civil Service only a short period after a comparable exercise had been carried out in Canada by the Glassco Commission (which reported in 1962). Yet the methods of work of the two bodies were quite different. Whereas the Glassco Commission adopted the customary procedure of inviting individuals and organizations to make submissions, it also organized its own research programme which involved the most extensive inquiry into the machinery of government ever undertaken in Canada. A total of 176 specialists from industry, the universities and the professions were engaged in the research. Approximately 21,000 days of work – the equivalent of eight man-years – were recorded by the research staff, exclusive of the related clerical work.[21] In contrast, the Fulton Committee appointed no research director, though Norman Hunt, one of the members of the Committee, was released for over a year from his duties as Fellow and Bursar of Exeter College, Oxford, so that he could devote his whole time to the work of the Committee. It commissioned a few research projects some of which were conducted in their spare time by academics in various universities – though the academics involved in its research were not invited formally to meet the Committee to explain their reports further or be questioned about their findings – and the Report itself appears to have been written by Norman Hunt[22] (a significant number of its main recommendations came from the management consultancy group he chaired).

As far as the present study is concerned, the most significant of the 158 recommendations in the Report can be grouped into five categories. First, there are the recommendations to overcome what is called the cult of the generalist (the often-held belief that the ideal administrator is a gifted layman who, moving frequently from job to job within the Service, can take a practical view of any problem, irrespective of subject matter, in the light of his knowledge and experience of the government machine). The Report states that 'the cult is obsolete at all levels and in all parts of the Service'. In the opinion of the Committee the Service must be quicker to recognise the contribution new professional skills can make to its work, for it has not always appreciated the need for new kinds of specialism quickly enough or recruited enough specialists of the high quality that the public interest demands, nor has it allowed the specialists to carry enough responsibility. The Committee said that in future it would not be enough for a 'generalist' civil servant to be expert in running the government machine, he must also acquire 'the basic concepts and knowledge whether social, economic, industrial or financial, relevant to his area of administration and appropriate to his level of responsibility'. This meant that a 'generalist' must specialise in the subject matter of his work (for example, some civil servants are doing work that is primarily economic and financial, others do work that is essentially social). The Committee recommended that in future the work should be distinguished into such types so that the civil servants can receive specially devised courses in relevant subjects and have their careers planned accordingly.

Secondly, the Committee made recommendations about the system of classes. It observed that there were forty-seven general service and similar classes with members distributed across the Service as a whole, and 1,400 departmental classes whose members work in one department only. Each civil servant is recruited on entry to a particular class, depending on the kind of work he applies for and his qualifications for it, and each class has its own career structure and separate pay scale. The Committee said that the system of classes therefore divides the Service 'both horizontally (between higher and lower in the same broad area of work) and vertically (between different skills, professions or disciplines). The Committee found that there is often no discernible difference in content between work done at the lower level of one class and the upper levels of the one beneath it. The system impedes the work of the Service, it hampers the Service in adapting itself to new tasks, prevents the best use of individual talent, contributes to the inequality of promotion prospects, causes frustration and resentment, and impedes the entry into wider management of those well fitted for it. The system of classes is too crude an instrument for the purpose of matching men to jobs and the word 'class' produces feelings of inferiority. The Committee therefore recommended that classes as such should be abolished. Instead, all civil servants should be organized in a single grading structure in which there are an appropriate number of different pay-levels matching different levels of skill and responsibility. This proposal would merge not only the Administrative, Executive and Clerical Classes, but also the Scientific Officer, Experimental Officer and Scientific Assistant Classes, the Works Group of Professional Classes, and the Architectural and Engineering

Draughtsman Classes. Equally, messengers, typists and machine operators would cease to belong to separate classes. However, at all levels where the work requires civil servants to specialise, 'occupational groups' would be needed. There would be a great variety of these, each engaged in a 'block of work . . . determined . . . by what is required for the most efficient achievement of its objectives' and civil servants would generally be recruited and trained as members of them. Such occupational groups would tend to develop their own career patterns and during the early years of a man's career the Committee expected he would remain within the specialism or group for which he was trained. Such a reorganization would imply the application of job-evaluation techniques which the Committee thought should be one of the tasks of the new Civil Service Department which it recommended.

Thirdly, the Committee made recommendations concerning specialists. It felt that many scientists, engineers and members of other specialist classes were not given the opportunity to exercise full authority for their work (partly because the policy and financial aspects of their work are reserved for a parallel group of 'generalist' administrators and partly because many specialists are equipped to practise only their own specialism. Although the Committee recommended that administrators should receive more specialised training, the Report states that they should not replace those specialists (e.g. engineers, accountants, economists, sociologists) whose primary concern is the practice of their specialism. The Report therefore recommended that specialists should be given more training in management and greater responsibilities; in each department the old concept of the gifted amateur would give way to one of greater specialisation and there would be a blend of administrators from various groups together with the various specialists.

Fourthly, the Report was critical of civil servants as managers because they were not adequately trained in management. The Committee said this criticism particularly applied to specialists, for it found that not enough scientists and other specialists had been trained for management, particularly personnel management, accounting and control. The Committee criticised career management in the Civil Service which, it said, was not sufficiently purposive or properly conceived, and civil servants were moved too frequently between unrelated jobs, often with little regard to personal preference or aptitude. It also said that the Service suffered from the remoteness of the Civil Service Commission from the Pay and Management group of divisions of the Treasury. It made a number of recommendations to overcome these difficulties including the setting up of a new Civil Service Department, special detailed recommendations for taking into account relevant qualifications during the recruitment process, and the creation of a Civil Service College to provide specialist training for administrators, courses in administration for specialists, and a large number of other courses for specialised purposes.

Fifthly, the Committee found there was not enough contact between the Civil Service and the rest of the community, partly because civil servants are expected to spend their entire working lives in the Service, and partly because the administrative process is surrounded by too much secrecy. The Committee recommended that there should be greater openness in a number of respects. The convention of anonymity should be modified, so that 'professional' administrators should be able to explain what they are doing in managing existing policies and implementing legislation. It also recommended greater mobility of staff into and out of the Service, less restrictive pension arrangements, late entry into the Service, more short service appointments and temporary exchange of staff with industry and commerce, nationalised industry and local government.

There have been a number of developments implementing its recommendations since the Report was published. On 26th June 1968, the day of publication, the Prime Minister made an important announcement in which he said that the Government accepted the proposal to establish a new Civil Service Department covering the previous responsibilities of the Pay and Management Divisions of the Treasury, and the Civil Service Commission. The new department was formally established from 1st November 1968. The Lord Privy Seal (Lord Shackleton) was appointed by the Prime Minister to assist him in the day-to-day operation of the Department, and the Permanent Secretary of the Civil Service Department has become the Official Head of the Home Civil Service.

The Prime Minister announced in the House of Commons Debate on the Fulton Report[23] that the Government had rejected the majority recommendation of the Committee that the selection of graduate entrants to administrative work should be deliberately weighted in favour of those whose university studies had been in subjects thought closely relevant to Civil Service work. This was further emphasised in the 1968 Annual Report of the Civil Service Commission which said: 'Our aim will be to continue to select the best people without regard to the subject of their first degree.'[24]

In the House of Commons Debate the Prime Minister also announced the setting up of an inquiry under Mr J. G. W. Davies (formerly secretary of the Cambridge University Appointments Board) into the Method II selection procedure for the administrative group of classes. That Committee, which reported in September 1969,[25] found that the method of selection was 'something to which the public service can point with pride', for it found no evidence of bias either in the procedures of selection or in the selectors themselves.

On the day of publication of the Fulton Report the Prime Minister also announced that a Civil Service College would be established. Later, in the Debate on the Report, he announced that as the total amount of college training would be very great, three centres would be needed. And it has since been announced that these are to be at the (non-residential) Centre for Administrative Studies, Regent's Park, plus two residential centres, at Sunningdale (in accommodation previously known as the Civil Defence College) and in Edinburgh. The established work of the Centre for Administrative Studies has already been developed and, for example, the course for Assistant Principals, previously lasting 20 weeks, has been extended to 28 weeks (with the additional time being spent on economic and social administration (2 weeks) and five different varieties of specialised 6-week courses).[26] On 26th June 1969 it was announced that Professor Eugene Grebenik, Professor of Social Studies in the University of Leeds, had been appointed Principal of the Civil Service College and would take up his appointment in January 1970, and that autumn 1970 was the intended date for opening the College.

Meanwhile, the Civil Service Department also announced that central management training in the Service had been increased by nearly 80 per cent in the training year 1968–69 including twice as much training for all classes at Principal level: and that considerably more use is already being made of external courses, for example at universities and business schools. In 1969–70 management training at Principal level will be redoubled and in addition there will be major increases in senior management seminars and courses.[27]

It was recognised that before some of the more detailed Fulton proposals on personnel management could be implemented, it was necessary to examine the work being performed by various groups of staff. To begin with, a detailed questionnaire has been sent to a sample of about 1,200 'administrators' between the grades of Higher Executive Officer and Assistant Secretary inclusive, 'designed to clarify and define the field in which they work, the kind of work they do within it and the kinds of knowledge and techniques that their jobs require'.[28] In addition, reviews are being made of present personnel management practices in selected Departments to accumulate knowledge about the way the Departments concerned post and train their staff, the extent to which they develop specialisation and move staff round, how far they aim to take the wishes of individuals into account, their promotion and reporting methods and procedures, and the extent to which the heads of operating divisions and branches are regarded as an integral part of the personnel management and promotion functions of the Department.

In order to increase mobility of staff whilst at the same time maintaining the Civil Service as predominantly a career Service, a new scheme was introduced in June 1968 for two-way interchanges between the Civil Service and industry and commerce, mainly at Principal level, and the first interchanges under it were made at the beginning of 1969. More and more opportunities are being provided for mature entrants into the Service: about one-third of the intake into the Principal grade in recent years have been late entrants (47 were recruited in this way in 1967, and about the same number in 1968).

Since the publication of the Fulton Report the Government has announced its proposals for a national earnings-related pensions scheme, which will affect many occupational schemes including the Civil Service. But as far as the Civil Service specifically is concerned, a special joint committee of the Staff and Official Sides of the National Whitley Council and the Joint Co-ordinating Committee for Government Industrial Establishments is at present reviewing the provisions of the Superannuation Acts and associated legislation.

A statement published in 1969 by the National Whitley Council Joint Committee on the Fulton Report made the assurance that:

'A high standard in the *working environment* . . . should be the aim. The re-organization of management within the Civil Service Department will mean that considerations of amenity in the working life of the civil servant will receive much more considered attention and high level support than has been possible in the past. Progress towards this aim will depend upon how soon the necessary resources can be made available, but the Civil Service Department will now be in a position to urge the "user" interest with vigour. The same applies to the provision of more extensive *secretarial assistance*.'²⁹

As far as reforming the Civil Service class structure is concerned, the Prime Minister announced the Government's decision on the day of publication of the Fulton Report: consultations with Staff Associations were to begin immediately with a view to working out a unified grading structure. And in August 1969 it was announced that progress was being made and it was hoped that an interim settlement on the problems posed by merging the Administrative, Executive and Clerical classes would be reached in 1970 and that the changes would come into effect in 1971. It was also announced that a scheme would shortly be introduced to establish 'a unified grading structure for the top of the Civil Service down to Under Secretary'.³⁰

On the question of openness and secrecy in the official bureaucracy, the Fulton Report welcomed the trend towards wider and more open consultation before decisions are to be taken and the increasing provision of detailed information on which decisions are made. In June 1969 the Government issued a White Paper, *Information and the Public Interest*,³¹ in which it agreed with the Fulton Committee in wishing to see more public explanation of administrative processes, a continuing trend towards more consultation before policy decisions are reached, and increasing participation by civil servants in explaining the work of Government to the public. The White Paper set out the results of an examination of the whole subject undertaken by the Government, highlighted examples of what had been done to improve consultation and demonstrated the considerable increase in the amount of factual and explanatory information provided by the Government. It stated: 'Much progress has already been made and departments are adopting a more liberal attitude towards the release of information than in the past'.

The Civil Service has also started to develop the concept of accountable management as recommended in the Fulton Report. Shortly after the Report was published departments were asked to survey their work for areas where complete accountability might be achieved, and make proposals for implementation. An inter-departmental committee was set up to establish a programme for developing accountable management (to examine pilot schemes started in the Royal Naval Supply and Transport Service, the Home Office, and H.M.S.O. – the Ministry of Defence has also been considering the introduction of more accountable management in its industrial units), examine the reports of surveys and proposals received from departments, and consider the problems involved in introducing accountable management in the Civil Service. In addition, the Civil Service Department is examining the work of the U.S. Bureau of the Budget on measuring productivity in Federal Government organizations, and has sent a member of the Department to study developments of this kind in the United States and Canada.

It has already been explained that the political environment is an important factor in understanding how the Civil Service works. It is, perhaps, an even more important factor in understanding how reforms of the administrative system are effected. In the last century there was considerable political pressure following the exposure of Crimean War administrative deficiencies. Similarly in the mid-twentieth century, the Labour Government of 1964 had been returned with an election programme of modernising Britain; there was a burst of publications analysing 'What's wrong with Britain'; and the administrative system was itself experiencing difficulties such as those connected with recruitment to the Administrative Class. This stimulated a growing concern which, together with certain institutional changes, seems to have brought about a change of attitudes within and in relation to the Civil Service. This is particularly impressive when, for example, all the post-Fulton changes are considered together (and not merely those mentioned here because of their significance for the higher Civil Service).

THE HIGHER CIVIL SERVANT: MACHINE OR MAN?

Writing at the beginning of this century, Graham Wallas observed that '. . . nearly all students of politics analyse institutions and avoid the analysis of man'.[32] Although the study of politics has developed so much since he wrote, his comment is still largely true of the study of that part we refer to as 'public administration'.

One reason is to be found in the background of the teachers of public administration; some have come from the public service itself with rather shallow knowledge of the other social sciences; others, with a more academic background, have been drawn towards the study of administrative institutions and their history. Another reason has been the difficulty of gaining access to material (and even where access has been granted it is sometimes given in such a way that it is more inhibiting than helpful), and the reputation of the central government service for refusing permission is such that some researchers are discouraged from worthy research without even knocking on the doors of a ministry. These and other factors have meant that public administration in Britain has not realised its opportunities: there has been a lack of appreciation of the contribution of certain approaches – economics, mathematics, and operational research as well as sociology – to the study of public administration problems. It is almost as if students of public administration have regarded these approaches as belonging to some different subject instead of studying their impact on management in the public service.

This is not to say, however, that the academic study of public administration is now wide open for development on new lines, though there is a noticeable movement in that direction. Perhaps the greatest change in recent years is that there is now some awareness of the significance of the knowledge we do not have. Consequently, the researches sponsored by the Fulton Committee have gained significance not so much from their size (often pitifully small and of questionable reliability) or their scope (often narrow and potentially unrepresentative of a vast Service with almost infinite tasks), but from the knowledge they suggested could be gained if the researchers had had the time and opportunities, and from being pioneering studies in a twilight area of the social sciences. And one of the most encouraging features of the post-Fulton Civil Service seems to be that research work has been expanded and leads then suggested followed up. It has already been mentioned that there is a major investigation in progress to clarify and define the field of work of Administrative civil servants – it was announced in February 1969 that a detailed questionnaire had been sent to a sample of 1,200 (later extended to over 2,000) 'administrators' between the grades of Higher Executive Officer and Assistant Secretary inclusive.[33] There has also been a survey of the Administrative, Executive, Scientific and Works Group Classes at Assistant Secretary and Principal level (some 1,800 questionnaires with interviews of some 250 respondents) to examine the possi-

L

bility of unified grading at those levels; and a survey (wholly by interview) of 180 posts at Under Secretary level and above for the purposes of establishing grades for the new grading structure. It is hoped that, in accordance with the trend towards more openness and less secrecy the Civil Service Department will in due course publish full details of these research projects.

This in turn has led to a number of significant consequences, not the least of which is a change of attitude within and a changed public image of the Civil Service. It has been revealed that the Service is not as bumbling as had been previously widely thought; but that some of its weaknesses are worse than imagined and often not sufficiently appreciated (for example, posting staff too frequently, and the lack of secretarial and/or supporting services). Furthermore, these seem now to be receiving urgent attention.

As for civil servants themselves, and in particular higher civil servants, they are tending to emerge from this experience as surprisingly human, with warts and all. One has the impression, for example, that Principals are the sort of people who would be popular holiday companions. They tend to have a keen, though somewhat cynical, sense of humour, wide interests, and could easily be conceded positions of leadership. They could make their mark in society, but this is often denied them by overwork, long hours, and the fatigue that results from it, all of which is largely unnecessary. Most higher civil servants work in central London, but outside office hours they may be separated from their work colleagues by sixty miles of metropolitan maze. Many feel themselves part of a classless sub-society, involved in a social process and identified with it; they have easy relations with all classes of people outside the Service.

Some higher civil servants chose their career because it is interesting, important, worthwhile work in the public service. Others, who might be caricatured as 'high Oxford' types, entered the Civil Service competitions for the fun of it, and then drifted into the Service because they were successful in the competitions. Most of them are not emotionally concerned with party politics, though they may get involved with issues; they feel that party loyalties become irrelevant when they are close to the working of government.

The fact remains, however, that higher civil servants occupy positions of considerable importance which affect the lives of everyone in the country. There is a sense in which they determine not only how policies should be effected, but also, to a very significant extent, which should be effected. Even in 1920, when the Civil Service was much smaller than it is today, Sidney and Beatrice Webb wrote that 'the government of Great Britain is in fact carried on not by the Cabinet nor even by the individual ministers, but by the Civil Service',[34] and Charles Aiken in the 1930s observed that 'the major social reforms are originated by the Civil Service'.[35] Although it is now generally accepted that any division of government into political and administrative activities is inadequate because the governing process is a seamless web of discretion and action, very few writers have been concerned with what might be called the practical aspects of government action and morality. Sir Henry Taylor might almost be writing today instead of in 1836, when he wrote: 'Amongst the writers on Government whose works my limited studies have entitled me to examine I have not met with any who have treated systematically of *Administrative* Government as it ought to be exercised in a free state.'[36]

Because so much attention has been given within the Service to the process of socialisation (and in the past relatively little attention has been paid to formal training) any understanding of the way higher civil servants behave must be concerned with understanding how this process works and what its consequences are. Political scientists have tended to be more concerned with the formal checks and balances that operate in institutions to ensure that no official has too much power. Perhaps more attention should now be paid to the informal aspects, to discovering codes of ethics which permeate administrative behaviour and act as a guide to the minutiae of everyday decisions. In our increasingly bureaucratic society this may be the core issue for further analysis in the latter part of the twentieth century.

Notes and Sources

1. Introduction

1. Graham Wallas, *Human Nature in Politics* (London, Constable, 1948), p. 268.

2. H. E. Dale, *The Higher Civil Service of Great Britain* (Oxford University Press, 1941). The useful book by Geoffrey K. Fry, *Statesmen in Disguise* (London, Macmillan, 1969), adopts a more institutional approach.

3. R. K. Kelsall, *Higher Civil Servants in Britain* (London, Routledge & Kegan Paul, 1955), p. 13.

4. T. A. Critchley, *The Civil Service Today* (London, Victor Gollancz, 1951), p. 74.

5. Tomlin Commission: *Royal Commission on the Civil Service 1929–31*, Report, Cmd. 3909, hereafter referred to as Tomlin Report (London, H.M.S.O.); Priestley Commission: *Royal Commission on the Civil Service 1953–1955*, Report, Cmd. 9613, hereafter referred to as Priestley Report (London, H.M.S.O.).

6. W. J. M. Mackenzie and J. W. Grove, *Central Administration in Britain* (London, Longmans, 1957).

7. Source: 'Introductory Factual memorandum on the Civil Service' in *The Civil Service, Vol. 4, Factual, Statistical and Explanatory Papers*, Evidence submitted to the Committee under the Chairmanship of Lord Fulton 1966–68, hereafter referred to as Fulton Report (London, H.M.S.O., 1968), p. 12.

8. *Evidence presented by the Association of First Division Civil Servants to the Committee on the Civil Service* (London, 1966).

9. Source: 'Introductory Factual memorandum on the Civil Service' in Fulton Report, Vol. 4, *Factual, Statistical and Explanatory Papers* (London, H.M.S.O., 1968), p. 38, and *Careers for Graduates, Posts in Government Service 1970* (London, Civil Service Commission, 1969).

10. Priestley Report, para. 15.

11. The Report of the Committee was not actually published, though details were released to the press. See, for example, *The Times* (12th July 1969).

2. Outline of Development

1. Graham Wallas, *Human Nature in Politics*, p. 263.

154

2. *The Indian Civil Service*, Report to the Right Hon. Sir Charles Wood, by T. B. Macaulay and others (the 'others' included Benjamin Jowett), (London, W. Thacker and Co, 1855), pp. 7–8.

3. For full details of how this happened see Sir Edward Blunt, *The I.C.S., The Indian Civil Service* (London, Faber and Faber, 1937).

4. According to T. F. Tout there is no earlier example of the familiar use of the phrase 'civil service', as applied to the officials of the British crown, than in the title of the Northcote-Trevelyan Report, and the establishment of the Civil Service Commission in 1855, to carry out the new plan of examinations made the term official. (T. F. Tout, *The English Civil Service in the Fourteenth Century*, Manchester University Press, 1916.) Dickens, who published in 1857, in *Little Dorrit*, his well-known denunciations of the Circumlocution Office and of the Barnacle Clan, never speaks of the civil service, though Mr Barnacle described himself as a 'public servant'. Trollope, however, who worked in the Post Office, uses the term Civil Service in *The Three Clerks*, which he published in 1858.

5. Phillip Woodruff, *The Men Who Ruled India*, 2 vols. (London, Jonathan Cape, 1953–54), Vol. 1, p. 115.

6. Sir Edward Blunt, *The I.C.S.*, p. 3.

7. Ibid., pp. 39–40.

8. Ibid., pp. 35–36.

9. *Hansard* (Commons, 10th July 1833), Vol. XIX, Third Series, Col. 525–526.

10. ' "I am to draw the Report", Macaulay writes on the 1st July 1854. "I must and will finish it in a week." He completed his rough draft on the 7th of July; wrote it out fair on Saturday the 8th; and read it to his brother-in-law on the Sunday. "Trevelyan", he says, "was well pleased"; and no wonder: for Macaulay had so framed his plan as to bring out all the strong points of the competitive system, and avoid its perils.' G. O. Trevelyan, *The Life and Letters of Lord Macaulay* (London, Longmans, 1883), Vol. II, p. 380.

11. Source: *The Selection and Training of Candidates for the Indian Civil Service*, C–1446 (London, H.M.S.O., 1876), p. 35.

12. Source: Ibid.

13. Source: Ibid.

14. Source: Ibid., p. 42.

15. *Royal Commission on Oxford and Cambridge Universities*, Report, Cmd. 1588 (London, H.M.S.O., 1922).

16. The Committee was appointed by a Treasury minute dated 12th April 1853, the text of which read:
'*Civil Service Commission*
'The Chancellor of the Exchequer states to the Board, that his attention

has been called to the inquiries which are in progress under the superintendence of the Treasury into the establishment of various public departments, for the purpose of considering applications for increase of salary, abolishing or consolidating redundant offices, supplying additional assistance where it is required, getting rid of obsolete processes, and introducing more simple and compendious modes of transacting business, establishing a proper distinction between intellectual and mechanical labour, and, generally, so revising and readjusting the public establishments as to place them on the footing best calculated for the efficient discharge of their important functions, according to the actual circumstances of the present time.

'In connection with these inquiries into each particular establishment, it is highly necessary that the conditions which are common to all the public offices, such as the preliminary testimonials of character and bodily health to be required from candidates for public employment, the examination into their intellectual attainments, and the regulation of the promotions, should be carefully considered, so as to attain every practicable security for the public that none but qualified persons will be appointed, and that they will afterwards have every practicable inducement to the active discharge of their duties.

'The general result of these inquiries and of the proceedings which will be taken upon them, will, undoubtedly, be that the public service will be conducted in a more efficient manner by a smaller number of persons than is the case at present. The gain in point of economy will probably be important. Five thousand pounds a year was saved by the recent revision of the Chief Secretary's Office, and the offices connected with it in London and Dublin; and the ultimate reduction of expenditure in consequence of the arrangements in progress at the Board of Trade will amount to upwards of five thousand pounds. But the gain in point of efficiency will be far greater. The object is, that the business of the public should be done in the best and most economical manner; and that arrangements of the public establishments which most conduces to this result will, in almost every case, be the most economical.

'Their Lordships' Assistant Secretary has of late years taken an active part in the Committees of Inquiry which have been appointed for this object, and it is desirable that the experience which he has acquired both as a member of these Committees and in the ordinary discharge of his duty at the Treasury, which is the central office for the revision of the public establishments, should be turned to the best account.

'The Chancellor of the Exchequer proposes that Sir Stafford Northcote, who acquired an extensive acquaintance with the public departments during his employment at the Board of Trade, and has proved on many occasions his superior fitness for administrative functions, should be joined with Sir

Charles Trevelyan in this important duty, and that he should give up his whole time to it. Sir Stafford Northcote has been already actively employed for some weeks, under their Lordships' appointment as a member of the Committee for inquiring into the contracts for the conveyance of the mails, and of the Committee for inquiring into the establishments of the Privy Council Office and the Board of Trade, and the departments of Practical Art and Science, and the other offices dependent upon the Board of Trade.

'My Lords entirely concur in the view which has been taken of this subject by the Chancellor of the Exchequer, and they are pleased to determine that Sir Stafford Northcote shall be paid at the rate of one thousand pounds a year for this service from the date of his first employment upon it, which salary will be paid from Civil Contingencies until further arrangements are made.

'Direct the Paymaster-General to pay Sir Stafford Northcote, in remuneration of his services as member of committees for inquiring into various public establishments with a view to a more efficient and economical performance of the public business, a salary of one thousand pounds a year until further orders, commencing on the 15th February last inclusively, and to charge the payments made by him under this direction to the account of Civil Contingencies.'

(*Parliamentary Papers 1854–5*, Vol. XXX, p. 375.)

17. *Royal Commission on Oxford and Cambridge Universities*, Report, para. 15.

18. See my articles 'Thomas Hill Green (1836–1882)', *The Review of Politics*, Vol. 27(1 965), pp. 516–531, and 'The Basis of T. H. Green's Philosophy', *International Review of History and Political Science*, Vol. 3 (1966), pp. 72–88. See also Melvin Richter, *The Politics of Conscience: T. H. Green and His Age:* (London, Weidenfeld & Nicolson, 1964).

19. Many of these men can be traced in Sir Ivo Elliott (Ed.), *The Balliol College Register 1833–1933* (Printed for private circulation, 1934): the register gives details of the careers of members of Balliol College during the heyday of the Oxford Idealists.

20. We should nowadays call his position Permanent Secretary of Her Majesty's Treasury.

21. Anthony Trollope, *An Autobiography* (London, Fontana Edition, 1962), p. 101.

22. Geoffrey Faber, *Jowett, a Portrait with a Background* (London, Faber & Faber, 1957), p. 176.

23. C. S. Parker, *Life and Letters of Sir James Graham*, Vol. 2, p. 210. Quoted in Emmeline Cohen, *The Growth of the British Civil Service* (London, Frank Cass, 1965), p. 85.

24. For example, 1855 was the date taken by the Tomlin Royal Commission, as the beginning of the civil service. See Tomlin Report, Cmd. 3909 (London, H.M.S.O.), para. 29.

25. Anthony Trollope, op. cit., pp. 42 and 46–47.

26. Edmund Yates, *His Reflections and Experiences* (Leipzig, Bernard Tauchnitz, 1885), Vol. I, p. 88.

27. Herbert Preston-Thomas, *The Work and Play of a Government Inspector* (London, Blackwood, 1909), pp. 1–2.

28. See above, note 16.

29. K. C. Wheare, *The Civil Service in the Constitution* (London, Athlone Press, 1954), pp. 7 and 10.

30. See *Reports of Committees of Inquiry into Public Offices and Papers Connected Therewith* (London, H.M.S.O., 1854).

31. Fulton Report, Vol. 1. *Report of the Committee 1966–68, Chairman: Lord Fulton* (London, H.M.S.O., 1968).

32. Quoted in Edward Hughes, 'Civil Service Reform 1853–5', *Public Administration*, 1954, Vol. 32, pp. 17–51.

33. Ibid., pp. 28–29.

34. Quoted in G. W. Keeton, *Trial by Tribunal* (London, Museum Press, 1960), p. 40.

35. 'Administrative Reform – The Civil Service', *Blackwood's Magazine* (1855), Vol. 78, pp. 116–134.

36. *Our Government Offices* (London, James Ridgway, 1855) – no author given.

37. Edward Hughes, op. cit., pp. 46–47.

38. Sir Stanley Leathes, 'Training of Public Servants', *Public Administration* (1923), Vol. I, pp. 343–362.

39. *Report of the Committee appointed to Consider and Report upon the Scheme of Examination for Class I of the Civil Service* (London, H.M.S.O., 1918), Parliamentary Papers 1517–18, viii, p. 129.

40. Fulton Report – *The Civil Service:* Vol. 1, *Report of the Committee 1966–68*; Vol. 2, *Report of the Management Consultancy Group*; Vol. 3, *Surveys and Investigations*; Vol. 4, *Factual, Statistical and Explanatory Papers*; Vol. 5, *Proposals and opinions* (London, H.M.S.O., 1968).

3. Recruitment

1. Graham Wallas, *Human Nature in Politics*, p. 262.

2. *Report on the Indian Civil Service*, (London H.M.S.O., 1854). Reprinted in Appendix B of The Fulton Report, Vol. 1, pp. 119–128.

3. Robert Moses, *The Civil Service of Great Britain* (New York, Columbia University & Longmans, 1914), p. 61.

4. A. Lawrence Lowell, *The Government of England* (New York, The Macmillan Company, 1908) p. 163.

5. *45th Report of the Civil Service Commissioners* (H.M.S.O., 1901).

6. A. Lawrence Lowell, *The Government of England*, p. 165.

7. MacDonnell Report – *Royal Commission on the Civil Service*, Cd. 6210 (London, H.M.S.O., 1912), *Minutes of Evidence*, q. 579.

8. Ibid., q. 715.

9. Ibid., q. 4,381.

10. Ibid., q. 22,299–22,372.

11. Ibid., q. 22,299–22,372.

12. Ibid., q. 24,922.

13. MacDonnell Commission, *Report*, para. 46.

14. MacDonnell Report, *Minutes of Evidence*, q. 2,169 and 2,711.

15. Ibid., q. 22,746.

16. Ibid., q. 1,766.

17. Ibid, q. 36,378.

18. J. F. Pickering, 'The Civil Service Unsuccessfuls: Fifteen Years Later', in The Fulton Report, Vol. 3(2), *Surveys and Investigations*, pp. 31–105.

19. Davies Report— *Report of the Committee of Inquiry into the Method II System of Selection (for the Administrative Class of the Home Civil Service)*, Cmnd. 4156 (London, H.M.S.O., 1965).

20. Ibid., p. 41.

21. Ibid., p. 4.

22. Press Release from Civil Service Department, 23rd May 1969.

23. 'Introductory Factual Memorandum on the Civil Service', The Fulton Report, Vol. 4, *Factual, Statistical and Explanatory Papers*, pp. 39–40.

24. Source: Ibid., p. 40.

25. This information is based on that given to the Fulton Committee in 'Selection Procedure for Civil Service Appointments', The Fulton Report, Vol. 4, *Factual, Statistical and Explanatory Papers*, pp. 297–331.

26. 'Memorandum No. 15 submitted by the Association of First Division Civil Servants', The Fulton Report, Vol. 5(1), *Proposals and Opinions*, pp. 105–121.

27. Source: Ibid., p. 117.

28. Source: Ibid., p. 116.

29. 'Selection Procedure for Civil Service Appointments', in The Fulton Report, Vol. 4, *Factual, Statistical and Explanatory Papers*, pp. 310–311.

30. 'The Civil Service Unsuccessfuls: Fifteen Years Later', in The Fulton Report, Vol. 3(2), *Surveys and Investigations*, pp. 31–105.

31. 'Profile of a Profession: The Administrative Class of the Civil

Service', in The Fulton Report, Vol. 3(2), *Surveys and Investigations*, pp. 1–29.

32. 'Recruitment of Graduates to the Civil Service: Survey of Student Attitudes', The Fulton Report, Vol. 3(2), *Surveys and Investigations*, p. 323.

33. See The Davies Report, Ch. 5.

34. G. K. Fry, *Statesmen in Disguise* (London, Macmillan, 1969).

35. 'Administrative Class Follow-up 1966', The Fulton Report, Vol. 3(2), *Surveys and Investigations*, H.M.S.O., 1968, p. 142.

36. The Davies Report, para. 5.35.

37. J. F. Pickering, 'Civil Service Unsuccessfuls: Fifteen Years Later', The Fulton Report, Vol. 3(2), *Surveys and Investigations*, pp. 31–105.

38. Ibid.

39. Richard A. Chapman, 'Profile of a Profession: the Administrative Class of the Civil Service', The Fulton Report, Vol. 3(2), pp. 1–29.

40. Eric Berne, *Games People Play* (London, André Deutsch, 1966).

41. 'Social Survey of the Civil Service', The Fulton Report, Vol. 3(1), *Surveys and Investigations*, pp. 36–37.

42. William Reid, 'Civil Service' in Robin Guthrie (Ed.) *Outlook, A Careers Symposium* (London, Macdonald, 1963).

43. 'Applications for the Administrative Class compared with University Output of Graduates in Groups of Subjects', The Fulton Report, Vol. 4, *Factual, Statistical and Explanatory Papers*, pp. 333–339.

44. The Davies Report, para. 4.7.

45. *Civil Service Commission, Annual Report*, London, 1968, p. 12.

46. 'Social Survey of the Civil Service', The Fulton Report, Vol. 3(1), *Surveys and Investigations*, p. 82.

4. *The Work They Do*

1. Graham Wallas, *Human Nature in Politics*, pp. 273–274.

2. William Reid, 'Civil Service', in Robin Guthrie (Ed.), *Outlook, A Careers Symposium*, p. 169. See also Robin McLaren, 'The Foreign Service', Ibid., pp. 139–144, and Camilla Crump, 'My Lady Mandarin', in Robin Guthrie and Tony Watts (Eds.), *Outlook Two, A Careers Symposium* (London, Macdonald, 1965), p. 65.

3. C. H. Sisson, *The Spirit of British Administration* (London, Faber, 1959), pp. 27–28.

4. The report based on this survey is 'Profile of a Profession', The Fulton Report, Vol. 3(2), *Surveys and Investigations*, pp. 1–29.

5. The Fulton Report, Vol. 2, *Report of a Management Consultancy Group*, para. 38.

6. Ibid., para. 39.

7. Ibid., para. 46.

8. Ibid., paras. 50–51.

9. The Association of First Division Civil Servants, Memorandum No. 15, The Fulton Report, Vol. 5(1), p. 119.

10. Ibid., Appendix III. The definition from the *Interim Report of the Reorganisation Committee (1921)*, para. 43, is also quoted in G. K. Fry, *Statesmen in Disguise*, p. 155.

11. *Royal Commission on the Civil Service, Appendix I to First Report of the Commissioner*, 1912, Q. 1,090–1.

12. C. K. Munro, *The Fountains in Trafalgar Square* (London, Heinemann, 1952), pp. 194–195.

13. See R. Douglas Brown, *The Battle of Crichel Down* (London, The Bodley Head, 1955), p. 102.

14. The Fulton Report, Vol. 2, p. 7.

15. See Memorandum No. 37, 'Comparative Costs of Training' submitted by H.M. Treasury to the Fulton Committee. The Fulton Report, Vol. 4, p. 553.

16. These were the report of an inter-departmental Working Party under the Chairmanship of Mr W. Morton, then Third Secretary on the Management side of the Treasury, which recommended that the formal training of Assistant Principals should be extended and that instead of the three-week course which they were receiving in the first year, they should be given a longer course in their third year of service. The second report was one prepared independently in the Economic Section of the Treasury which suggested that a course of about 13 weeks in economics and statistics might be given for administrators in 'economic' Departments. See The Fulton Report, Vol. 4, p. 524.

17. The Fulton Report, Vol. 4, p. 527.

18. Source: Ibid., p. 533.

19. Ibid., p. 532.

20. Ibid., p. 534.

21. The Fulton Report, Vol. 2, p. 20.

22. C. K. Munro, *The Fountains in Trafalgar Square*, p. ix.

23. C. H. Sisson, *The Spirit of British Administration*.

24. R. K. Kelsall, *Higher Civil Servants in Britain*.

25. G. K. Fry, *Statesmen in Disguise*.

26. C. K. Munro, *The Fountains in Trafalgar Square*, pp. 28–29.

5. *The Environment for Work*

1. Graham Wallas, *Human Nature in Politics*, p. 274.

2. During the survey for 'Profile of a Profession'.

3. For example, the evidence given by the Association of First Division Civil Servants, The Fulton Report, Vol. 5(1), pp. 105–134.

4. Quoted in the evidence to the Fulton Committee from the Association of First Division Civil Servants.

5. The Davies Report, p. 28.

6. See evidence to the Fulton Committee from W. J. L. Plowden, N. D. Deakin and J. B. L. Mayall, The Fulton Report, Vol. 5(2), pp. 998–1,005.

7. Evidence to the Fulton Committee, The Fulton Report, Vol. 4, pp. 645–649.

8. Nikolaus Pevsner, *Buildings of England*; London, Vol. 1 (1957), p. 472. Quoted by Anthony Sampson, *Anatomy of Britain* (London, Hodder & Stoughton, 1962), p. 232.

9. W. J. L. Plowden et al, in The Fulton Report, Vol. 5(2), pp. 998–1,005.

10. Reported in *The Times*, 12th May 1967.

11. Reported in *The Times*, 29th June 1968.

12. The Fulton Report, Vol. 5(1), p. 128.

13. This definition is based on that given in O. Glenn Stahl, *Public Personnel Administration* (New York, Harper & Row, 1956, fifth edition).

14. W. J. L. Plowden et al, in The Fulton Report, Vol. 5(2), p. 999.

15. Reported in *The Times*, June 1968.

16. During the survey for 'Profile of a Profession'.

17. The Fulton Report, Vol. 5(1), p. 296 and p. 288.

18. Ibid., p. 290.

19. T. H. Profitt, 'Great Britain', in F. F. Ridley (Ed.), *Specialists and Generalists* (London, Allen & Unwin, 1968).

20. 'Social Survey on the Civil Service', The Fulton Report, Vol. 3(1), *Surveys and Investigations*, p. 44.

21. Ibid., p. 46.

22. Source: Ibid., pp. 25–26.

23. Ibid., p. 27.

24. *Sixth Report from the Estimates Committee together with the Minutes of the Evidence taken before Sub-Committee E, Session 1964–65, Recruitment to the Civil Service*, HC 308 (H.M.S.O., 1965), q. 474–475.

25. Ibid., q. 720–721.

26. Ibid., q. 472.

27. H. E. Dale, *The Higher Civil Service of Great Britain*, p. 161.

28. Sir Edward Bridges, *Portrait of a Profession, The Civil Service Tradition* (Cambridge University Press, 1950).

29. Ibid., p. 16.

30. Ibid., pp. 22–23.

31. Reported in *The Times*, 29th June 1968.

32. R. J. S. Baker, 'Discussion and Decision-Making in the Civil Service', *Public Administration* (1953), Vol. 41, pp. 345–356.

33. H. E. Dale, *The Higher Civil Service of Great Britain*, p. 64.

34. W. L. George, *Blind Alley* (London, T. Fisher Unwin Ltd, 1919), p. 20.

35. Anthony Sampson, *Anatomy of Britain*, p. 228.

36. C. P. Snow, *The Listener*, Vol. LVII, pp. 619–620 (18th April 1957). Quoted by Anthony Sampson, *Anatomy of Britain*, p. 221.

37. C. P. Snow, *Corridors of Power* (London, Macmillan, 1964; Penguin edition, 1966, p. 25).

38. The Fulton Report, Vol. 1, para. 15.

39. During the 1960s a number of books were published on this general theme, most of them not particularly good. They included: Andrew Hill and Anthony Whichelow, *What's Wrong with Parliament?*, Rex Malik, *What's Wrong with British Industry?*, Gerda Cohen, *What's Wrong with Hospitals?*, Nick Earle, *What's Wrong with the Church?* (all published by Penguin Books, 1964), Peter Shore, *Entitled to Know* (MacGibbon and Kee, 1966), Andrew Shonfield, *Modern Capitalism, the changing balance of public and private power* (Oxford University Press, 1965), Brian Chapman, *British Government Observed* (Allen and Unwin, 1963), Bernard Crick, *The Reform of Parliament* (Weidenfeld and Nicolson, 1964), Max Nicholson, *The System: The Misgovernment of Modern Britain* (Hodder and Stoughton, 1967).

40. *Sixth Report from the Estimates Committee together with the Minutes of the Evidence taken before Sub-Committee E, session 1964–65, Recruitment to the Civil Service*, HC 308, q. 829.

41. Ibid., q. 830.

42. Ibid., p. 7.

43. Ibid., q. 49.

44. A comment during the survey for 'Profile for a Profession'.

6. *Life outside the Office*

1. Graham Wallas, *The Nature of Politics*, p. 279.

2. 'Social Survey of the Civil Service', The Fulton Report, Vol. 3(1), *Surveys and Investigations*, p. 12.

3. Ibid., p. 42.

4. H. E. Dale, *The Higher Civil Service of Great Britain*, p. 29.

5. 'Social Survey of the Civil Service', The Fulton Report, Vol. 3(1), *Surveys and Investigations*, p. 28.

6. Ibid., p. 31.

7. H. E. Dale, *The Higher Civil Service of Great Britain*, pp. 107–108.

8. C. K. Munro, *The Fountains of Trafalgar Square*, p. 94.

9. H. E. Dale, *The Higher Civil Service of Great Britain*, p. 107.

10. See, for example, the evidence of the Labour Party (The Fulton Report, Vol. 5(2), pp. 652–673).

11. Anthony Sampson, *Anatomy of Britain*, p. 234.

12. Ibid., p. 235.

13. C. P. Snow, *The Corridors of Power*, p. 40.

14. D. L. Mumby, 'Memorandum No. 136', The Fulton Report, Vol. 5(2), pp. 982–983.

15. *The Times*, 13th October 1969.

16. C. K. Munro, *The Fountains in Trafalgar Square*, pp. 200–201.

17. J. P. Mallalieu, *Passed to You, Please* (London, Victor Gollancz, 1942).

18. R. K. Kelsall, *Higher Civil Servants in Britain*.

19. 'Social Survey of the Civil Service', The Fulton Report, Vol. 3(1), *Surveys and Investigations*, p. 51.

20. Ibid., pp. 35 and 52.

21. H. E. Dale, *The Higher Civil Service of Great Britain*, p. 44.

22. Source: *Sixth Report from the Estimates Committee, together with the Evidence taken before Sub-Committee E, and Appendices. Session 1964–65. Recruitment to the Civil Service*, HC 308 (H.M.S.O., 1965), p. 31.

23. Ibid., p. 31.

24. Source: The Fulton Report, Vol. 5(2), p. 927.

25. H. E. Dale, *The Higher Civil Service of Great Britain*, Ch. 4.

26. Ibid., p. 76.

27. Lord Salter, *Memoirs of a Public Servant* (London, Faber & Faber, 1961), p. 71.

7. *Conclusion*

1. Graham Wallas, 'Government', Inaugural address to the Institute of Public Administration for the session 1927–28. Published in *Public Administration*, 1928, Vol. VI, pp. 3–15. Reprinted in *Men and Ideas, Essays by Graham Wallas* (London, Allen & Unwin, 1940), pp. 114–130.

2. Memorandum No. 38 submitted to the Fulton Committee by The Institution of Professional Civil Servants, The Fulton Report, Vol. 5(1), *Proposals and Opinions*, pp. 294–346.

3. See *Sixth Report from the Estimates Committee together with the Minutes of the Evidence taken before Sub-Committee E and Appendices*, q. 807. Also quoted in William Plowden, 'The Civil Service—Industry Swap', *New Society*, 7th March 1968, p. 344.

4. Sir Edward Bridges, *Portrait of a Profession, The Civil Service Tradition*, p. 25.

5. Marshall E. Dimock, *A Philosophy of Administration* (New York, Harper & Row, 1958), Ch. 7.

6. J. J. Deutsch, 'Some Thoughts on the Public Service', an informal address to the annual meeting of the Ottawa Chapter of the Canadian Political Science Association, later published in the *Canadian Journal of Economics and Political Science*, Vol. 23 (1957), pp. 183–191, and reprinted in J. E. Hodgetts and D. C. Corbett, *Canadian Public Administration* (Toronto, The Macmillan Company of Canada, 1960), pp 297–304.

7. Lord Bridges in *Whitehall and Beyond*, Three conversations with Norman Hunt with a comment by Lord Bridges (B.B.C., 1964), p. 64.

8. See Sir Hilton Poynton, 'The Civil Service and Parliament', Memorandum No. 140 submitted to the Fulton Committee, The Fulton Report, Vol. 5(2), *Proposals and Opinions*, pp. 1,005–1,011. Also R. J. S. Baker, 'Discussion and Decision-making in the Civil Service', *Public Administration*, Vol. 41 (1963), pp. 345–356.

9. W. L. Plowden et al, in The Fulton Report, Vol. 5(2), *Proposals and Opinions*, p. 1,002.

10. Ibid., p. 1,002.

11. The Fulton Report, Vol. 1, *Report of the Committee, 1966–68*, para. 150.

12. See *First Report from the Select Committee on Procedure, Session 1968–69, together with the proceedings of the Committee, minutes of evidence, appendices and index, Scrutiny of Public Expenditure and Administration*, HC 410 (London, H.M.S.O., 1969), p. 27.

13. *Sixth Report from the Estimates Committee together with the Minutes of the Evidence taken before Sub-Committee E and Appendices*, q. 757.

14. *Report of the Committee on the Political Activities of Civil Servants*, The Masterman Report, Cmd. 7718 (H.M.S.O., 1949), para. 92.

15. A Fabian Group, *The Administrators* (The Fabian Society, 1964).

16. The Fulton Report, Vol. 1, *Report of the Committee, 1966–68*, Ch. 8.

17. *Information and the Public Interest*, Cmnd. 4089 (H.M.S.O., 1969).

18. 13th April 1969.

19. Andrew Shonfield, 'The Pragmatic Illusion', Gaitskell Memorial Lecture, Nottingham University, 1967, printed in *Encounter* (June 1967).

20. See *Whitehall and Beyond*, Jo Grimond, Enoch Powell, Harold Wilson, three conversations with Norman Hunt, with a comment by Lord Bridges.

21. See *Royal Commission on Government Organisation*, 5 vols. (Ottawa, Queen's Printer, 1962). Also G. V. Tunnock, 'The Glassco Commission: did it cost more than it was worth?', *Canadian Public Administration*, Vol. 7, (1964), pp. 389–397.

22. See Preface to The Fulton Report, Vol. 1, *Report of the Committee 1966–68*, also *The Observer*, 30th June 1968.

23. 21st November 1968.

24. Civil Service Commission, *Annual Report 1968* (H.M.S.O., 1969), p. 10.

25. The Davies Report.

26. Civil Service National Whitley Council, *Developments on Fulton*, 1969.

27. Information Release from Civil Service Department, 26th June 1969.

28. Civil Service National Whitley Council, *Developments on Fulton*.

29. Ibid., p. 23.

30. Information Release from Civil Service Department, 28th August 1969.

31. Cmnd. 4089.

32. Graham Wallas, *Human Nature in Politics*, p. 37.

33. Civil Service National Whitley Council, *Developments on Fulton*, pp. 16–17.

34. S. and B. Webb, *A Constitution for the Socialist Commonwealth of Great Britain* (London, Longmans Green, 1920), p. 67.

35. Charles Aiken, 'The British Bureaucracy and the Origin of Parliamentary Policy II', *American Political Science Review* Vol. 33 (1939), p. 225.

36. Sir Henry Taylor, *The Statesman* (New York, Mentor Books, 1958), p. 23.

Bibliography

This bibliography is in three sections, a selection of books and articles of relevance to matters discussed in the text of this book, full references to official documents, and a list of the contents of the five volumes of the Fulton Report.

BOOKS AND ARTICLES

ABBOTT, Evelyn and CAMPBELL, Lewis *The Life and Letters of Benjamin Jowett*, 3 vols. (London, John Murray, 1897).

AIKEN, Charles, 'The British Bureaucracy and the Origins of Parliamentary Policy (I and II)', *The American Political Science Review* (1939), Vol. 33, pp. 26–46 and 219–233.

ALLEN, C. K., *Bureaucracy Triumphant* (London, Oxford University Press, 1931).

ANONYMOUS, 'Administrative Reform—The Civil Service', *Blackwood's Magazine* (1855), Vol. 78, pp. 116–134.

ANONYMOUS, *Our Government Offices* (London, James Ridgway, 1855).

BAKER, R. J. S., 'Discussion and Decision-Making in the Civil Service', *Public Administration* (1953) Vol. 41, pp. 345–356.

BALCHIN, Nigel M., *The Small Back Room* (London, Collins, 1943).

BERNE, Eric, *Games People Play* (London, André Deutsch, 1966).

BEVERIDGE, Lord, *Power and Influence* (London, Hodder & Stoughton, 1953).

BLAU, Peter M., *Bureaucracy in Modern Society* (New York, Random House, 1956).

BLUNT, Sir Edward, *The I.C.S., The Indian Civil Service* (London, Faber & Faber, 1937).

BOTTOMORE, T. B., *Elites and Society* (London, C. A. Watts, 1964).

BOYLE, Andrew, *Montagu Norman* (London, Cassell, 1967).

BRIDGES, Sir Edward, *Portrait of a Profession, The Civil Service Tradition*, (London, Cambridge University Press, 1950).

BRIDGES, Lord, *The Treasury* (London, Allen & Unwin, 1964).

BRITTAN, Samuel, *The Treasury Under the Tories, 1951–1964* (London, Penguin Books, 1964).

BROWN, R. Douglas, *The Battle of Crichel Down* (London, The Bodley Head, 1955).

BROWN, R. G. S., 'Organization Theory and Civil Service Reform', *Public Administration* (1965), Vol. 43, pp. 313–330.

BURNS, C. Delisle, *Whitehall* (London, Oxford University Press, 1921).

CAMPBELL, G. A., *The Civil Service in Britain* (London, Duckworth, 1965, 2nd. Ed.).

CARR-SAUNDERS, A. M., *Professions, Their Organization and Place in Society* (Oxford, The Clarendon Press, 1928).

CHAPMAN, Brian, *British Government Observed* (London, Allen & Unwin, 1963).

CHAPMAN, Brian, *The Profession of Government* (London, Allen & Unwin, 1959).

CHAPMAN, Richard A., 'Thomas Hill Green (1836–1882)', *The Review of Politics*, Vol. 27 (1965), pp. 516–531.

CHAPMAN, Richard A., 'The Basis of T. H. Green's Philosophy', *International Review of History and Political Science*, Vol. 3 (1966), pp. 72–88.

CHAPMAN, Richard A., *Decision Making* (London, Routledge & Kegan Paul, 1969).

CHAPMAN, Richard A., 'The Fulton Report: A Summary', *Public Administration*, Vol. 46 (1968), pp. 443–451.

CHESTER, D. N. and WILLSON, F. M. G. *The Organisation of British Central Government* (London, Allen & Unwin, 1968, 2nd. Ed.).

Civil Service National Whitley Council, *Developments on Fulton* (London, C.S.N.W.C., 1969).

CLAY, Sir Henry, *Lord Norman* (London, Macmillan, 1957).

COHEN, Emmeline, *The Growth of the British Civil Service, 1780–1939* (London, Allen & Unwin, 1941; Reprinted by Frank Cass, 1965).

COHEN, Gerda, *What's Wrong with Hospitals?* (London, Penguin Books, 1964).

COLE, Taylor, *The Canadian Bureaucracy* (Durham, N.C., Duke University Press, 1949).

CRICK, Bernard, *The Reform of Parliament* (London, Weidenfeld & Nicolson, 1964).

CRITCHLEY, Thomas A., *The Civil Service Today* (London, Victor Gollancz, 1951).

CRUMP, Camilla, 'My Lady Mandarin' in Robin Guthrie (Ed.), *Outlook Two, A Careers Symposium* (London, Macdonald, 1965).

DALE, H. E., *The Personnel and Problems of the Higher Civil Service* (London, Oxford University Press, 1943).

DALE, H. E., *The Higher Civil Service of Great Britain* (London, Oxford University Press, 1941).

DALE, J. R., *The Clerk in Industry* (Liverpool University Press, 1962).

DE SAUTOY, Peter, *The Civil Service* (London, Oxford University Press, 1957).

DEUTSCH, J. J., 'Some Thoughts on the Public Service' in J. E. Hodgetts and D. C. Corbett, *Canadian Public Administration* (Toronto, The Macmillan Company of Canada, 1960).

DICKENS, Charles, *Little Dorrit* (London, Bradbury & Evans, 1857).

DIMOCK, Marshall E., *A Philosophy of Administration* (New York, Harper & Row, 1958).

DODD, C. H., 'Recruitment to the Administrative Class, 1960–1964', *Public Administration* (1967), Vol. 45, pp. 55–80.

EARLE, Nick, *What's Wrong with the Church?* (London, Penguin Books, 1964).

EATON, Dorman B., *Civil Service in Great Britain* (New York, Harper & Brothers, 1880).

ELLIOTT, Sir Ivo (Ed.), *The Balliol College Register, 1833–1933* (Printed for private circulation, 1934).

EMDEN, C. S., *The Civil Servant in the Law and the Constitution* (London, Stevens, 1923).

FABER, Geoffrey, *Jowett, A Portrait with a Background* (London, Faber & Faber, 1957).

FABIAN GROUP, A, *The Administrators* (London, The Fabian Society, 1964).

FARNELL, Lewis R., *An Oxonian Looks Back* (London, Martin Hopkinson Ltd, 1934).

FINER, H., *British Civil Service* (London, The Fabian Society and Allen & Unwin, 1937).

FINER, S. E., *The Life and Times of Sir Edwin Chadwick* (London, Methuen, 1952).

FRANCKS, Sir Oliver S., *The Experiences of a University Teacher in the Civil Service* (London, Oxford University Press, 1947).

FRY, G. K., *Statesmen in Disguise* (London, Macmillan, 1969).

GAWTHROP, Louis C., *Bureaucratic Behaviour in the Executive Branch* (New York, The Free Press, 1969).

GEORGE, W. L., *Blind Alley* (London, T. Fisher Unwin Ltd, 1919).

GLADDEN, E. N., *Civil Services of the United Kingdom* (London, Frank Cass, 1967).

GREAVES, H. R. G., *The Civil Service in the Changing State* (London, George G. Harrap, 1947).

GRIFFITH, Wyn, *The British Civil Service, 1854–1954* (London, H.M.S.O., 1954).

HARROD, Sir Roy, *The Life of John Maynard Keynes* (London, Macmillan, 1951).

M*

HILL, Andrew and WICHELOW, Anthony, *What's Wrong with Parliament?* (London, Penguin Books, 1964).

HUGHES, Edward, 'Civil Service Reform 1853–55', *Public Administration* (1954), Vol. 32, pp. 17–51.

HUNT, Norman, *Whitehall and Beyond. Three conversations with Norman Hunt (Jo Grimond, Enoch Powell, Harold Wilson), with a comment by Lord Bridges* (London, B.B.C., 1964).

KARL, Frederick R., *C. P. Snow: The Politics of Conscience* (Southern Illinois University Press, 1963).

KEETON, George W., *Trial by Tribunal* (London, Museum Press, 1960).

KEITH, A. B., *A Constitutional History of India, 1600–1935* (London, Methuen, 1936).

KELLY, Sir David, *The Ruling Few* (London, Hollis & Carter, 1952).

KELSALL, R. K., *Higher Civil Servants in Britain* (London, Routledge & Kegan Paul, 1955).

KEMPE, Sir John Arrow, *Reminiscences of an Old Civil Servant, 1846–1927* (London, John Murray, 1928).

LANG, Andrew, *Life, Letters and Diary of Sir Stafford Northcote, First Earl of Iddesleigh* (London, Blackwood, 1891).

LEATHES, Sir Stanley, 'Training of Public Servants', *Public Administration* (1923), Vol. 1, pp. 343–362.

LEWIS, Roy and MAUDE, A. E. U., *The English Middle Classes* (London, Penguin Books, 1953).

LOWELL, A. Lawrence, *The Government of England* (New York, The Macmillan Company, 1908).

MACKENZIE, W. J. M., and GROVE, J. W., *Central Administration in Britain* (London, Longmans, 1957).

MALIK, Rex, *What's Wrong with British Industry?* (London, Penguin Books, 1964).

MALLALIEU, J. P., *Passed to You, Please* (London, Victor Gollancz, 1942).

MCGREGOR, Douglas, *The Professional Manager* (New York, McGraw-Hill, 1967).

MCLAREN, Robin, 'The Foreign Service', in Robin Guthrie (Ed.), *Outlook, A Careers Symposium* (London, Macdonald, 1963).

MERTON, Robert K. (Ed.), *Reader in Bureaucracy* (Glencoe, The Free Press, 1952).

MILLAR, Robert, *The New Classes* (London, Longmans, 1966).

MISES, Ludwig Von, *Bureaucracy* (New Haven, Yale University Press, 1944).

MONCK, Bosworth, *How the Civil Service Works* (London, Phoenix House, 1952).

MONIER-WILLIAMS, Sir M. et al, *Memorials of Old Haileybury College*, (London, Constable, 1894).

MORRISON, Herbert, *Government and Parliament* (Oxford University Press, 1954).

MOSES, Robert, *The Civil Service of Great Britain* (New York, Columbia University and Longmans, 1914).

MUNRO, C. K., *The Fountains in Trafalgar Square* (London, Heinemann, 1952).

MUSTOE, Nelson E., *The Law and Organization of the British Civil Service* (London, Pitman, 1932).

NICHOLSON, Max, *The System: The Misgovernment of Modern Britain* (London, Hodder & Stoughton, 1967).

O'MALLEY, L. S. S., *The Indian Civil Service, 1601–1930* (London, John Murray, 1931).

PARRIS, Henry, *Constitutional Bureaucracy* (London, Allen & Unwin, 1969).

PICKERING, J. F., 'Recruitment to the Administrative Class, 1960–1964: Part 2', *Public Administration* (1967), Vol. 45, pp. 169–199.

PLOWDEN, William, 'The Civil Service—Industry Swap', *New Society*, (7th March 1968), p. 334.

PRESTON-THOMAS, Herbert, *The Work and Play of a Government Inspector* (London, Blackwood, 1909).

PROFFITT, T. H., 'Great Britain' in F. F. Ridley (Ed.), *Specialists and Generalists* (London, Allen & Unwin, 1968).

RAYNOR, John, *The Middle Class* (London, Longmans, 1969).

READER, W. J., *Professional Men* (London, Weidenfeld & Nicolson, 1966).

REID, William, 'Civil Service', in Robin Guthrie (Ed.), *Outlook, A Careers Symposium* (London, Macdonald, 1963).

RICHTER, Melvin, *The Politics of Conscience: T. H. Green and His Age* (London, Weidenfeld & Nicolson, 1964).

RIDLEY, F. F. (Ed.), *Specialists and Generalists* (London, Allen & Unwin, 1968).

ROBSON, William A. (Ed.), *The Civil Service in Britain and France* (London, Hogarth Press, 1956).

ROBSON, William A., *From Patronage to Proficiency in the Public Service* (London, The Fabian Society, 1922).

SALTER, Lord, *Memoirs of a Public Servant* (London, Faber & Faber, 1961).

SALTER, Lord, *Slave of the Lamp, A Public Servant's Notebook* (London, Weidenfeld & Nicolson, 1967).

SAMPSON, Anthony, *Anatomy of Britain* (London, Hodder & Stoughton, 1962).

SCOTT, Sir Harold, *Your Obedient Servant* (London, André Deutsch, 1959).

SELF, Peter, *Bureaucracy or Management?* (London, G. Bell & Sons Ltd, 1965).

SHONFIELD, Andrew, *Modern Capitalism, the changing balance of public and private power* (London, Oxford University Press, 1965).

SHONFIELD, Andrew, 'The Pragmatic Illusion', *Encounter* (June, 1967).

SHORE, Peter, *Entitled to Know* (London, MacGibbon & Kee, 1966).

SISSON, C. H., *The Spirit of British Administration* (London, Faber & Faber, 1959).

SMELLIE, Kingsley B., *A Hundred Years of English Government* (London, Duckworth, 1937).

SNOW, C. P., *Corridors of Power* (London, Macmillan, 1964; Penguin Books, 1966).

SNOW, C. P., *Science and Government* (Cambridge, Massachusetts, Harvard University Press, 1960).

SNOW, C. P., 'The Corridors of Power', *The Listener* (1957), Vol. LVII, pp. 619–620.

STAHL, O. Glenn, *Public Personnel Administration* (New York, Harper & Row, 1956, fifth edition).

STANLEY, David T., *The Higher Civil Service, An Evolution of Federal Personnel Practices* (Washington, The Brookings Institution, 1964).

TAYLOR, Henry, *The Statesman* (New York, Mentor Books, 1958).

THOMAS, Hugh (Ed.), *Crisis in the Civil Service* (London, Anthony Blond, 1968).

THOMAS, Hugh (Ed.), *The Establishment* (London, Anthony Blond, 1959).

TOUT, T. F., *The English Civil Service in the Fourteenth Century* (Manchester University Press, 1916).

TREVELYAN, G. O., *The Life and Letters of Lord Macaulay*, 2 vols. (London, Longmans, 1883).

TROLLOPE, Anthony, *An Autobiography* (London, Fontana, 1962).

TROLLOPE, Anthony, *The Three Clerks* (London, Oxford University Press, 1907).

TUCKWELL, W., *Reminiscences of Oxford* (London, Cassell, 1900).

TUNNOCK, G. V., 'The Glassco Commission: did it cost more than it was worth?', *Canadian Public Administration* (1964), Vol. 7, pp. 389–397)

VICKERS, Sir Geoffrey, *The Art of Judgement: A Study of Policy Making* (London, Chapman & Hall, 1965).

WALKER, Nigel, *Morale in the Civil Service* (Edinburgh University Press, 1961).

WALLAS, Graham, *Human Nature in Politics* (London, Constable, 1948).

WALLAS, Graham, *Men and Ideas, Essays by Graham Wallas* (London, Allen & Unwin, 1940).

WEBB, S. and B., *A Constitution for the Socialist Commonwealth of Great Britain* (London, Longmans Green, 1920).

WHEARE, K. C., *The Civil Service in the Constitution* (London, The Athlone Press, 1954).

WOODRUFF, Phillip, *The Men Who Ruled India*, 2 vols. (London, Jonathan Cape, 1953–54).

WRIGHT, Maurice, *Treasury Control of the Civil Service, 1854–1874* (London, Oxford University Press, 1969).

YATES, Edmund, *His Reflections and Experiences* (Leipzig, Bernard Tauchnitz, 1885).

OFFICIAL REPORTS

Reports of Committees of Inquiry into Public Offices and Papers Connected Therewith (London, H.M.S.O., 1854).

The Indian Civil Service, Report to the Right Hon. Sir Charles Wood, by T. B. Macaulay and others (London, W. Thacker and Co, 1855).

The Selection and Training of Candidates for the Indian Civil Service, Cmd. 1446 (London, H.M.S.O., 1876).

Royal Commission on the Civil Service: The MacDonnell Report, Cmd. 6210 (London, H.M.S.O., 1912).

Report of the Committee appointed to Consider and Report upon the Scheme of Examination for Class I of the Civil Service, Parliamentary Papers, 1517–18, viii (London, H.M.S.O., 1918).

Royal Commission on Oxford and Cambridge Universities Report, Cmd. 1588 (London, H.M.S.O., 1922).

Royal Commission on the Civil Service, 1929–31: The Tomlin Report, Cmd. 3909 (London, H.M.S.O., 1931).

Report of the Committee on the Political Activities of Civil Servants: The Masterman Report, Cmd. 7718 (London, H.M.S.O., 1949).

Royal Commission on the Civil Service, 1953–55: The Priestley Report, Cmd. 9613 (London, H.M.S.O., 1955).

Report of the Royal Commission on Government Organization: The Glassco Report, 5 vols. (Ottawa, The Queen's Printer, 1962).

Sixth Report from the Estimates Committee, together with the minutes of the Evidence taken before Sub-Committee E, Session 1964–65, Recruitment to the Civil Service, HC. 308 (London, H.M.S.O., 1965).

The Civil Service, Vol. 1, Report of the Committee, 1966–68; Vol. 2, Report of the Management Consultancy Group; Vol. 3, Surveys and Investigations; Vol. 4, Factual, statistical, and explanatory papers; Vol. 5, Proposals and opinions: The Fulton Report, Cmnd. 3638 (London, H.M.S.O., 1968–69).

Information and the Public Interest, Cmnd. 4089 (London, H.M.S.O., 1969).

Report of the Committee of Inquiry into the Method II System of Selection (for the Administrative Class of the Home Civil Service): The Davies Report, Cmnd. 4156 (London, H.M.S.O., 1965).

Civil Service Commission, Annual Report, 1968 (London, Civil Service Commission, 1969).

First Report from the Select Committee on Procedure, Session 1968–69, together with the proceedings of the Committee, minutes of evidence, appendices and index, Scrutiny of Public Expenditure and Administration, HC. 410 (London, H.M.S.O., 1969).

THE FULTON REPORT

Vol. 1   *Report of the Committee, 1966–68* (Cmnd. 3638)
[Members of the Committee: Lord Fulton (Chairman), Sir Norman Kipping, G.C.M.C., K.B.E., J.P., Sir Philip Allen, K.C.B., Mr W. C. Anderson, C.B.E., Rt Hon. Sir Edward Boyle, Bart., M.P., Sir William Cook, C.B., F.R.S., Sir James Dunnett, K.C.B., C.M.G., Dr Norman Hunt, Mr R. R. Neild, Mr R. Sheldon, M.P., Professor Lord Simey, Sir John Wall, O.B.E.]

Vol. 2   *Report of a Management Consultancy Group*

Vol. 3 (1) *Survey and Investigations*:
Social Survey of the Civil Service: Memorandum submitted by A. H. Halsey and I. M. Crewe

Vol. 3 (2) *Surveys and Investigations*:

Memorandum No. 2   Profile of a Profession, by Dr Richard A. Chapman

Memorandum No. 3   Civil Service Unsuccessfuls, by Dr J. F. Pickering

Memorandum No. 4   Administrative Class Follow-up Survey, by Dr E. Anstey

Memorandum No. 5   Executive Class Follow-up Survey, by The Civil Service Commission

Memorandum No. 6   School Backgrounds of Members of the Administrative class, by H.M. Treasury

Memorandum No. 7   Survey of Wastage of Executive and Clerical Officers, by H.M. Treasury

Memorandum No. 8   Study of Ability, Efficiency and Job Satisfaction among Executive and Clerical Officers, by H.M. Treasury

Memorandum No. 9   Recruitment of Graduates: Survey of Student Attitudes, by the Psychological Research Centre

Memorandum No. 10 Reports on the Civil Service since the Northcote-Trevelyan Report, by Mr J. B. Bourn

Vol. 4 (1) *Factual, Statistical and Explanatory Papers:*

Memorandum No. 1	Introductory Factual Memorandum on the Civil Service, by H.M. Treasury
Memorandum No. 2	Civil Service Manpower Statistics, by H.M. Treasury
Memorandum No. 3	Number of Staff in the Civil Service 1964 to 1967, by H.M. Treasury
Memorandum No. 4	Numbers of Civil Servants in Various Classes and Departments 1929 to 1966, by H.M. Treasury
Memorandum No. 5	Computers and the Size of the Civil Service, by H.M. Treasury
Memorandum No. 6	Civil Service – Demand for Manpower, by H.M. Treasury
Memorandum No. 7	Civil Service – Demand for Manpower, by H.M. Treasury
Memorandum No. 8	Output of the Educational System: Destinations óf School-leavers, by The Department of Education and Science
Memorandum No. 9	Selection Procedure for Civil Service Appointments, by The Civil Service Commission
Memorandum No. 10	Composition of the Final Selection Board, by The Civil Service Commission
Memorandum No. 11	Applications for the Administrative Class Compared with University Output of Graduates in Groups of Subjects, by H.M. Treasury and the Civil Service Commission
Memorandum No. 12	Successful Candidates in Method II from Universities other than Oxford and Cambridge, by The Civil Service Commission
Memorandum No. 13	Age-Spread of Assistant Principals, by The Civil Service Commission
Memorandum No. 14	The Quality of Recent Executive Class Recruitments, and a Comparison with Pre-war Standards, by The Civil Service Commission
Memorandum No. 15	Proportion of Established Entrants to the Scientific Officer Class with Higher Degrees, by H.M. Treasury

Vol. 4   Memorandum No. 16 Ministry of Labour Cadets, by The Ministry of Labour

Memorandum No. 17 Recruitment of Women to the Civil Service by H.M. Treasury

Memorandum No. 18 Establishment, by H.M. Treasury

Memorandum No. 19 Establishment Procedure, by H.M. Treasury

Memorandum No. 20 Temporary Status, by H.M. Treasury

Memorandum No. 21 Retirement Policy, by H.M. Treasury

Memorandum No. 22 Retirements under Section 9, 10 and 45 of the Superannuation Act, 1965, by H.M. Treasury

Memorandum No. 23 Civil Servants on Secondment, by H.M. Treasury

Memorandum No. 24 Loan of Principals from Industry, Commerce and Universities, by H.M. Treasury

Memorandum No. 25 The Acceptance of Business Appointments by Civil Servants, by H.M. Treasury

Memorandum No. 26 Fringe Benefits and Certain Miscellaneous Provisions, by H.M. Treasury

Memorandum No. 27 Political Activities of Civil Servants, by H.M. Treasury

Memorandum No. 28 Departmental Classes, by H.M. Treasury

Memorandum No. 29 Number of Classes with their own P.R.U. Surveys, by H.M. Treasury

Memorandum No. 30 List of General Service, Linked Departmental and Departmental Grades for which there is Formal Representation in the Non-Industrial Civil Service, by H.M. Treasury

Memorandum No. 31 Whitleyism

Memorandum No. 32 Civil Service Training, by H.M. Treasury

Memorandum No. 33 Treasury Centre for Administrative Studies and Management Training at Principal and Assistant Secretary Level, by H.M. Treasury

Memorandum No. 34 Sabbatical Leave in the Home Civil Service, by H.M. Treasury

Memorandum No. 35 External Training, Further Education and Study and Sabbatical Leave, by H.M. Treasury

Vol. 4   Memorandum No. 36 Complementing and Training Margins, by H.M. Treasury

Memorandum No. 37 Comparative Costs of Training, by H.M. Treasury

Memorandum No. 38 Promotion in the Administrative and Executive Classes, by H.M. Treasury

Memorandum No. 39 Departmental Promotion Practices, by H.M. Treasury

Memorandum No. 40 Patterns of Administrative Class Careers, by H.M. Treasury with notes by Home Office, Ministry of Housing and Local Government and Ministry of Power

Memorandum No. 41 Administrative Class – Proportion of Direct Entrants Reaching Assistant Secretary and Above, by H.M. Treasury

Memorandum No. 42 Wastage of Principals and Assistant Principals, by H.M. Treasury

Memorandum No. 43 Entry into the Administrative Class After the Normal Age, by H.M. Treasury

Memorandum No. 44 Previous Histories of Permanent Secretaries, by H.M. Treasury

Memorandum No. 45 Origins of the Senior Executive Staff in the Ministry of Labour, by the Ministry of Labour

Memorandum No. 46 Management of the Civil Service, by H.M. Treasury

Memorandum No. 47 The Management of the Scientific Officer Class, by H.M. Treasury

Memorandum No. 48 The Works Group, by H.M. Treasury

Memorandum No. 49 Management Services, by H.M. Treasury

Memorandum No. 50 Management of the Civil Service: The Organization and Functions of the Treasury, by H.M. Treasury

Memorandum No. 51 Management Accounting Unit, by H.M. Treasury

Memorandum No. 52 Relationship between Organization and Methods and Staff Inspection, by H.M. Treasury

Memorandum No. 53 Operational Research, by H.M. Treasury

Memorandum No. 54 A.D.P. in the Civil Service, by H.M. Treasury

Vol. 4 Memorandum No. 55 The Adequacy of the Provision of Office Machines in the Civil Service, by H.M. Treasury

Memorandum No. 56 Government Office Accommodation, by The Ministry of Public Building and Works

Vol. 5 (1) *Proposals and Opinions*:

Memorandum No. 1 The Future Structure of the Civil Service, by H.M. Treasury

Memorandum No. 2 The Clerical Classes, by H.M. Treasury

Memorandum No. 3 The Management Group – Promotion Opportunities, by H.M. Treasury

Memorandum No. 4 Selection for the Management Group by Academic Examinations, by H.M. Treasury and The Civil Service Commission

Memorandum No. 5 The Scientific Classes in the Civil Service, by H.M. Treasury

Memorandum No. 6 Works Group, Allied and Supporting Classes, by H.M. Treasury

Memorandum No. 7 Engineers, Scientists and the Works Group, by H.M. Treasury

Memorandum No. 8 Economist, Statistician, and Research Officer Classes, by H.M. Treasury

Memorandum No. 9 Professional Accountants, by H.M. Treasury

Memorandum No. 10 The Legal Class, by H.M. Treasury

Memorandum No. 11 Supporting Grades, by H.M. Treasury

Memorandum No. 12 Departmental Classes, by H.M. Treasury

Memorandum No. 13 Management Training in the Civil Service by H.M. Treasury

Memorandum No. 14 Central Management of the Civil Service, by the Head of the Home Civil Service

Memorandum No. 15 Introduction, by the Association of First Division Civil Servants

Memorandum No. 16 By the Association of First Division Civil Servants

Memorandum No. 17 The Museum Keeper Class, by The Association of First Division Civil Servants

Memorandum No. 18 Statistician and Economist Classes by The Association of First Division Civil Servants

Vol. 5 (1) Memorandum No. 19 By The Association of Government Supervisors and Radio Officers

Memorandum No. 20 Introduction, by The Association of H.M. Inspectors of Taxes (A.I.T.)

Memorandum No. 21 By The Association of Officers of the Ministry of Labour

Memorandum No. 22 Introduction – the C.S.C.A., by The Civil Service Clerical Association

Memorandum No. 23 By The Civil Service Clerical Association

Memorandum No. 24 Personnel Management, by The Civil Service Clerical Association

Memorandum No. 25 By The Civil Service Clerical Association

Memorandum No. 26 The Future Structure of the Legal Civil Service, by the Civil Service Legal Society

Memorandum No. 27 By The Civil Service Union

Memorandum No. 28 Introduction, by The County Court Officers' Association

Memorandum No. 29 By The Customs and Excise Controlling Grade Association

Memorandum No. 30 By The Customs and Excise Federation

Memorandum No. 31 By The Customs and Excise Federation

Memorandum No. 32 By The Customs and Excise Launch Service Association

Memorandum No. 33 Introduction, by The Customs and Excise Preventive Staff Association

Memorandum No. 34 The Future Structure of the Customs and Excise Department in the Civil Service, by The Customs and Excise Surveyors' Association

Memorandum No. 35 By The Inland Revenue Staff Federation

Memorandum No. 36 Comment on H.M. Treasury's Note 'The Future Structure of the Civil Service', by The Institution of Professional Civil Servants

Memorandum No. 37 Civil Service Organization: Some Issues for Consideration, by The Institution of Professional Civil Servants

Memorandum No. 38 Introduction, by The Institution of Professional Civil Servants

Memorandum No. 39 A Social Scientist Group, by The Institution of Professional Civil Servants

N

Vol. 5 (1) Memorandum No. 40 The I.P.C.S. Proposal for a Social Scientist Group, by H.M. Treasury

Memorandum No. 41 Rejoinder to the Treasury Note on the Proposal for a Social Scientist Group by The Institution of Professional Civil Servants

Memorandum No. 42 Comparative Career Values of Administrative, Works Group and Scientific Officer Classes, by The Institution of Professional Civil Servants

Memorandum No. 43 Comparative Career Values of the Administrative, Works Group and Scientific Officer Classes, by H.M. Treasury

Memorandum No. 44 Comparative Career Values of the Administrative, Works Group, and Scientific Officer Classes: Comment on the Treasury's Note, by The Institution of Professional Civil Servants

Memorandum No. 45 Professional Accountants, by The Institution of Professional Civil Servants

Memorandum No. 46 The Future Structure, Recruitment and Training, with Particular Emphasis on the Regional and Local Office requirements of the Employment Service of the Ministry of Labour, by The Ministry of Labour Staff Association

Memorandum No. 47 Introduction, by The Society of Civil Servants

Memorandum No. 48 Introduction, by The Society of Civil Servants

Memorandum No. 49 By The Society of Technical Civil Servants

Vol. 5 (2) *Proposals and Opinions*:

Memorandum No. 50 Memorandum, by The Accepting Houses Committee and The Issuing Houses Association

Memorandum No. 51 The Role of Professional Accountants in the Civil Service, by The Accountants Joint Parliamentary Committee

Memorandum No. 52 Salaries of Articled Clerks, by The Accountants Joint Parliamentary Committee

Vol. 5 (2) Memorandum No. 53 By The Association of Child Care Officers
Memorandum No. 54 By The Association of Education Committees
Memorandum No. 55 By The Association of Family Caseworkers
Memorandum No. 56 By The Association of Municipal Corporations
Memorandum No. 57 By The Association of Unit Trust Managers
Memorandum No. 58 By The British Electrical and Allied Manufacturers' Association
Memorandum No. 59 By British European Airways
Memorandum No. 60 By The British Institute of Management
Memorandum No. 61 By The British Insurance Association
Memorandum No. 62 By The British National Export Council
Memorandum No. 63 By The British Railways Board
Memorandum No. 64 By The Building Societies Association
Memorandum No. 65 By The Chartered Land Societies Committee
Memorandum No. 66 By The Committee of Directors of Research Associations
Memorandum No. 67 By The Confederation of British Industry
Memorandum No. 68 Problems of Recruitment, by The Confederation of British Industry
Memorandum No. 69 Exchanges between the Civil Service and Industry, by The Confederation of British Industry
Memorandum No. 70 By The Conference of the Electronics Industry
Memorandum No. 71 By The Consumer Council
Memorandum No. 72 By The Council of Engineering Institutions
Memorandum No. 73 By The County Councils Association
Memorandum No. 74 Senior Administrative Posts in the Scottish Education Department, by The Educational Institute of Scotland
Memorandum No. 75 By The Scottish Education Department
Memorandum No. 76 By The Electricity Council
Memorandum No. 77 By The Engineers' Guild Limited
Memorandum No. 78 'Irregular' Appointments to the Higher Civil Service Since October, 1964, by The Fabian Society

Vol. 5 (2) Memorandum No. 79 By The Greater London Council
Memorandum No. 80 By *The Guardian*
Memorandum No. 81 By The Eastern Regional Hospital Board (Scotland)
Memorandum No. 82 By The Manchester Regional Hospital Board
Memorandum No. 83 By The North East Metropolitan Regional Hospital Board
Memorandum No. 84 By The Oxford Regional Hospital Board
Memorandum No. 85 By The Sheffield Regional Hospital Board
Memorandum No. 86 By The Welsh Hospital Board
Memorandum No. 87 By The Incorporated Society of Auctioneers and Landed Property Agents
Memorandum No. 88 By The Institute of Biology
Memorandum No. 89 By The Institute of Cost and Works Accountants
Memorandum No. 90 By The Institute of Landscape Architects
Memorandum No. 91 Employment of Professional Accountants in the Civil Service, by The Institute of Municipal Treasurers and Accountants
Memorandum No. 92 By The Institute of Personnel Management
Memorandum No. 93 By The Institute of Physics and The Physical Society
Memorandum No. 94 By The Institution of Heating and Ventilating Engineers
Memorandum No. 95 By International Computers and Tabulators Limited
Memorandum No. 96 By The International Publishing Corporation
Memorandum No. 97 By The Labour Party
Memorandum No. 98 By The Liberal Party
Memorandum No. 99 By The National Citizens' Advice Bureaux Council
Memorandum No. 100 By The National Coal Board
Memorandum No. 101 By The National Council of Social Service
Memorandum No. 102 By The Operational Research Society
Memorandum No. 103 By The Rating and Valuation Association
Memorandum No. 104 By The Royal Institute of British Architects

Vol. 5 (2) Memorandum No. 105 By The Ministry of Public Building and Works

Memorandum No. 106 By The Royal Institute of Chemistry

Memorandum No. 107 By The Royal Institute of Public Administration

Memorandum No. 108 By The Royal Society

Memorandum No. 109 By The Royal Statistical Society

Memorandum No. 110 By Headmasters and Headmistresses of Schools

Memorandum No. 111 By The Science Research Council

Memorandum No. 112 By Shell International Petroleum Company Limited

Memorandum No. 113 By The Society of British Aerospace Companies Limited

Memorandum No. 114 By The Stock Exchange

Memorandum No. 115 By The Trades Union Congress

Memorandum No. 116 By The United Kingdom Atomic Energy Authority

Memorandum No. 117 By The Central Youth Employment Executive summarising the views of Youth Employment Officers

Memorandum No. 118 By Mr R. G. S. Brown

Memorandum No. 119 By Mr J. W. P. Chidell

Memorandum No. 120 By Professor B. R. Crick and Mr W. Thornhill

Memorandum No. 121 By Dr T. L. Cottrell

Memorandum No. 122 By Sir George Dunnett, K.B.E., C.B.

Memorandum No. 123 By Dr A. F. Earle

Memorandum No. 124 By a Group of Members of the Economic Planning Staff of the Ministry of Overseas Development

Memorandum No. 125 By Sir Donald Gibson, C.B.E.

Memorandum No. 126 By Mr J. H. T. Goldsmith, C.B.E.

Memorandum No. 127 By Mr J. H. T. Goldsmith, C.B.E.

Memorandum No. 128 By a Group of Members of the Association of First Division Civil Servants

Memorandum No. 129 By Mr L. J. Harris

Memorandum No. 130 State Service – Manpower Considerations by Mr C. E. Horton, C.B.E.

Memorandum No. 131 By Sir Herbert Hutchinson, K.B.E., C.B.

Memorandum No. 132 Whitehall's Brain Drain, by Mr P. Jay

Memorandum No. 133 By Mr N. Johnson

Vol. 5 (2) Memorandum No. 134 By Mr W. J. T. Knight
          Memorandum No. 135 Engineers in the Civil Service, by Mr E. M'Ewen
          Memorandum No. 136 By Mr D. L. Munby
          Memorandum No. 137 By Sir Anthony Percival, C.B.
          Memorandum No. 138 By Sir Edward Playfair, K.C.B.
          Memorandum No. 139 By Mr W. J. L. Plowden, Mr N. D. Deakin and Mr J. B. L. Mayall
          Memorandum No. 140 The Civil Service and Parliament, by Sir Hilton Poynton, G.C.M.G.
          Memorandum No. 141 Evidence of Principals on Loan from Industry, Commerce and Universities
          Memorandum No. 142 International Aspects of the Functions of the Home Civil Service, by Dr Roy Pryce
          Memorandum No. 143 By Mr J. H. Robertson
          Memorandum No. 144 The Role of the Civil Service in Modern Society, by Mr W. S. Ryrie
          Memorandum No. 145 By Mr D. Seers
          Memorandum No. 146 The Use of Economists in the Ministry of Agriculture, Fisheries and Food, by Ministry of Agriculture, Fisheries and Food
          Memorandum No. 147 By Professor P. J. Self
          Memorandum No. 148 The Civil Service Pension System, by Mr I. S. T. Senior, Mr E. A. French, and Mr A. Axon
          Memorandum No. 149 By a Senior Executive Officer
          Memorandum No. 150 By Mr Trevor Smith on behalf of the Acton Society Trust
          Memorandum No. 151 By Mr F. Stacey
          Memorandum No. 152 The Scientific Civil Service, by Sir Frank Turnbull, K.B.E., C.B., C.I.E., Dr A. V. Cohen, and Dr H. T. Hookway
          Memorandum No. 153 The Future of the Centre of Administrative Studies, by Mr B. Turvey.

Index

Numbers in italic indicate Notes